I0176472

ENGLISH
NORWEGIAN

THEME-BASED
DICTIONARY

Contains over 3000 commonly
used words

Theme-based dictionary British English-Norwegian - 3000 words
British English collection

By Andrey Taranov

T&P Books vocabularies are intended for helping you learn, memorize and review foreign words. The dictionary is divided into themes, covering all major spheres of everyday activities, business, science, culture, etc.

The process of learning words using T&P Books' theme-based dictionaries gives you the following advantages:

- Correctly grouped source information predetermines success at subsequent stages of word memorization
- Availability of words derived from the same root allowing memorization of word units (rather than separate words)
- Small units of words facilitate the process of establishing associative links needed for consolidation of vocabulary
- Level of language knowledge can be estimated by the number of learned words

T&P Books Publishing
www.tpbooks.com

ISBN: 978-1-78492-018-0

This book is also available in E-book formats.
Please visit www.tpbooks.com or the major online bookstores.

NORWEGIAN THEME-BASED DICTIONARY
British English collection

T&P Books vocabularies are intended to help you learn, memorize, and review foreign words. The vocabulary contains over 3000 commonly used words arranged thematically.

- Vocabulary contains the most commonly used words
- Recommended as an addition to any language course
- Meets the needs of beginners and advanced learners of foreign languages
- Convenient for daily use, revision sessions, and self-testing activities
- Allows you to assess your vocabulary

Special features of the vocabulary

- Words are organized according to their meaning, not alphabetically
- Words are presented in three columns to facilitate the reviewing and self-testing processes
- Words in groups are divided into small blocks to facilitate the learning process
- The vocabulary offers a convenient and simple transcription of each foreign word

The vocabulary has 101 topics including:

Basic Concepts, Numbers, Colors, Months, Seasons, Units of Measurement, Clothing & Accessories, Food & Nutrition, Restaurant, Family Members, Relatives, Character, Feelings, Emotions, Diseases, City, Town, Sightseeing, Shopping, Money, House, Home, Office, Working in the Office, Import & Export, Marketing, Job Search, Sports, Education, Computer, Internet, Tools, Nature, Countries, Nationalities and more ...

TABLE OF CONTENTS

Pronunciation guide	8
Abbreviations	10

BASIC CONCEPTS	11
1. Pronouns	11
2. Greetings. Salutations	11
3. Questions	12
4. Prepositions	12
5. Function words. Adverbs. Part 1	13
6. Function words. Adverbs. Part 2	14

NUMBERS. MISCELLANEOUS	16
7. Cardinal numbers. Part 1	16
8. Cardinal numbers. Part 2	17
9. Ordinal numbers	17

COLORS. UNITS OF MEASUREMENT	18
10. Colours	18
11. Units of measurement	18
12. Containers	19

MAIN VERBS	21
13. The most important verbs. Part 1	21
14. The most important verbs. Part 2	21
15. The most important verbs. Part 3	22
16. The most important verbs. Part 4	23

TIME. CALENDAR	25
17. Weekdays	25
18. Hours. Day and night	25
19. Months. Seasons	26

TRAVEL. HOTEL   29

20. Trip. Travel   29
21. Hotel   29
22. Sightseeing   30

TRANSPORT   32

23. Airport   32
24. Aeroplane   33
25. Train   33
26. Ship   34

CITY   37

27. Urban transport   37
28. City. Life in the city   38
29. Urban institutions   39
30. Signs   40
31. Shopping   41

CLOTHING & ACCESSORIES   43

32. Outerwear. Coats   43
33. Men's & women's clothing   43
34. Clothing. Underwear   44
35. Headwear   44
36. Footwear   44
37. Personal accessories   45
38. Clothing. Miscellaneous   45
39. Personal care. Cosmetics   46
40. Watches. Clocks   47

EVERYDAY EXPERIENCE   48

41. Money   48
42. Post. Postal service   49
43. Banking   49
44. Telephone. Phone conversation   50
45. Mobile telephone   51
46. Stationery   51
47. Foreign languages   52

MEALS. RESTAURANT   54

48. Table setting   54
49. Restaurant   54
50. Meals   54
51. Cooked dishes   55
52. Food   56

53. Drinks   58
54. Vegetables   59
55. Fruits. Nuts   60
56. Bread. Sweets   60
57. Spices   61

PERSONAL INFORMATION. FAMILY   62

58. Personal information. Forms   62
59. Family members. Relatives   62
60. Friends. Colleagues   63

HUMAN BODY. MEDICINE   65

61. Head   65
62. Human body   66
63. Diseases   66
64. Symptoms. Treatments. Part 1   68
65. Symptoms. Treatments. Part 2   69
66. Symptoms. Treatments. Part 3   70
67. Medicine. Drugs. Accessories   70

FLAT   72

68. Flat   72
69. Furniture. Interior   72
70. Bedding   73
71. Kitchen   73
72. Bathroom   74
73. Household appliances   75

THE EARTH. WEATHER   76

74. Outer space   76
75. The Earth   77
76. Cardinal directions   78
77. Sea. Ocean   78
78. Seas & Oceans names   79
79. Mountains   80
80. Mountains names   81
81. Rivers   81
82. Rivers names   82
83. Forest   82
84. Natural resources   83
85. Weather   84
86. Severe weather. Natural disasters   85

FAUNA   87

87. Mammals. Predators   87
88. Wild animals   87

89. Domestic animals 88
90. Birds 89
91. Fish. Marine animals 91
92. Amphibians. Reptiles 91
93. Insects 92

FLORA 93

94. Trees 93
95. Shrubs 93
96. Fruits. Berries 94
97. Flowers. Plants 95
98. Cereals, grains 96

COUNTRIES OF THE WORLD 97

99. Countries. Part 1 97
100. Countries. Part 2 98
101. Countries. Part 3 98

PRONUNCIATION GUIDE

Letter	Norwegian example	T&P phonetic alphabet	English example
Aa	plass	[a], [ɑ:]	bath, to pass
Bb	bøtte, albue	[b]	baby, book
Cc [1]	centimeter	[s]	city, boss
Cc [2]	Canada	[k]	clock, kiss
Dd	radius	[d]	day, doctor
Ee	rett	[e:]	longer than in bell
Ee [3]	begå	[ɛ]	man, bad
Ff	fattig	[f]	face, food
Gg [4]	golf	[g]	game, gold
Gg [5]	gyllen	[j]	yes, New York
Gg [6]	regnbue	[ŋ]	English, ring
Hh	hektar	[h]	humor
Ii	kilometer	[ı], [i]	tin, see
Kk	konge	[k]	clock, kiss
Kk [7]	kirke	[h]	humor
Jj	fjerde	[j]	yes, New York
kj	bikkje	[h]	humor
Ll	halvår	[l]	lace, people
Mm	middag	[m]	magic, milk
Nn	november	[n]	name, normal
ng	id_langt	[ŋ]	English, ring
Oo [8]	honning	[ɔ]	bottle, doctor
Oo [9]	fot, krone	[u]	book
Pp	plomme	[p]	pencil, private
Qq	sequoia	[k]	clock, kiss
Rr	sverge	[r]	rice, radio
Ss	appelsin	[s]	city, boss
sk [10]	skikk, skyte	[ʃ]	machine, shark
Tt	stør, torsk	[t]	tourist, trip
Uu	brudd	[y]	fuel, tuna
Vv	kraftverk	[v]	very, river
Ww	webside	[v]	very, river
Xx	mexicaner	[ks]	box, taxi
Yy	nytte	[ı], [i]	tin, see
Zz [11]	New Zealand	[s]	star, cats
Ææ	vær, stær	[æ]	chess, man
Øø	ørn, gjø	[ø]	eternal, church
Åå	gås, værhår	[o:]	fall, bomb

Comments

[1] before **e, i**
[2] elsewhere
[3] unstressed
[4] before **a, o, u, å**
[5] before **i** and **y**
[6] in combination **gn**
[7] before **i** and **y**
[8] before two consonants
[9] before one consonant
[10] before **i** and **y**
[11] in loanwords only

ABBREVIATIONS
used in the dictionary

English abbreviations

ab.	-	about
adj	-	adjective
adv	-	adverb
anim.	-	animate
as adj	-	attributive noun used as adjective
e.g.	-	for example
etc.	-	et cetera
fam.	-	familiar
fem.	-	feminine
form.	-	formal
inanim.	-	inanimate
masc.	-	masculine
math	-	mathematics
mil.	-	military
n	-	noun
pl	-	plural
pron.	-	pronoun
sb	-	somebody
sing.	-	singular
sth	-	something
v aux	-	auxiliary verb
vi	-	intransitive verb
vi, vt	-	intransitive, transitive verb
vt	-	transitive verb

Norwegian abbreviations

f	-	feminine noun
f pl	-	feminine plural
m	-	masculine noun
m pl	-	masculine plural
m/f	-	masculine, neuter
m/f pl	-	masculine/feminine plural
m/f/n	-	masculine/feminine/neuter
m/n	-	masculine, feminine
n	-	neuter
n pl	-	neuter plural
pl	-	plural

BASIC CONCEPTS

1. Pronouns

I, me	jeg	['jæj]
you	du	[dʉ]
he	han	['hɑn]
she	hun	['hʉn]
it	det, den	['de], ['den]
we	vi	['vi]
you (to a group)	dere	['derə]
they	de	['de]

2. Greetings. Salutations

Hello! (fam.)	Hei!	['hæj]
Hello! (form.)	Hallo! God dag!	[hɑ'lʉ], [gʉ 'dɑ]
Good morning!	God morn!	[gʉ 'mɔːn]
Good afternoon!	God dag!	[gʉ'dɑ]
Good evening!	God kveld!	[gʉ 'kvɛl]
to say hello	å hilse	[ɔ 'hilsə]
Hi! (hello)	Hei!	['hæj]
greeting (n)	hilsen (m)	['hilsən]
to greet (vt)	å hilse	[ɔ 'hilsə]
How are you? (form.)	Hvordan står det til?	['vʉːdɑn stoːr de til]
How are you? (fam.)	Hvordan går det?	['vʉːdɑn gor de]
What's new?	Hva nytt?	[vɑ 'nʏt]
Goodbye! (form.)	Ha det bra!	[hɑ de 'brɑ]
Bye! (fam.)	Ha det!	[hɑ 'de]
See you soon!	Vi ses!	[vi sɛs]
Farewell!	Farvel!	[far'vɛl]
to say goodbye	å si farvel	[ɔ 'si far'vɛl]
Cheers!	Ha det!	[hɑ 'de]
Thank you! Cheers!	Takk!	['tɑk]
Thank you very much!	Tusen takk!	['tʉsən tɑk]
My pleasure!	Bare hyggelig	['bɑrə 'hʏgeli]
Don't mention it!	Ikke noe å takke for!	['ikə 'nʉe ɔ 'tɑkə for]
It was nothing	Ingen årsak!	['iŋən 'oːʂɑk]
Excuse me! (fam.)	Unnskyld, ...	['ʉn‚sʏl ...]
Excuse me! (form.)	Unnskyld meg, ...	['ʉn‚sʏl me ...]
to excuse (forgive)	å unnskylde	[ɔ 'ʉn‚sʏlə]
to apologize (vi)	å unnskylde seg	[ɔ 'ʉn‚sʏlə sæj]

My apologies	Jeg ber om unnskyldning	[jæj ber ɔm 'ʉn‚ʂyldniŋ]
I'm sorry!	Unnskyld!	['ʉn‚ʂyl]
to forgive (vt)	å tilgi	[ɔ 'til‚ji]
It's okay! (that's all right)	Ikke noe problem	['ikə 'nʉe prʉ'blem]
please (adv)	vær så snill	['vær ʂɔ 'snil]
Don't forget!	Ikke glem!	['ikə 'glem]
Certainly!	Selvfølgelig!	[sɛl'følgəli]
Of course not!	Selvfølgelig ikke!	[sɛl'følgəli 'ikə]
Okay! (I agree)	OK! Enig!	[ɔ'kɛj], ['ɛni]
That's enough!	Det er nok!	[de ær 'nɔk]

3. Questions

Who?	Hvem?	['vɛm]
What?	Hva?	['va]
Where? (at, in)	Hvor?	['vʉr]
Where (to)?	Hvorhen?	['vʉrhen]
From where?	Hvorfra?	['vʉrfra]
When?	Når?	[nɔr]
Why? (What for?)	Hvorfor?	['vʉrfʉr]
Why? (~ are you crying?)	Hvorfor?	['vʉrfʉr]
What for?	Hvorfor?	['vʉrfʉr]
How? (in what way)	Hvordan?	['vʉ:dɑn]
What? (What kind of ...?)	Hvilken?	['vilkən]
Which?	Hvilken?	['vilkən]
To whom?	Til hvem?	[til 'vɛm]
About whom?	Om hvem?	[ɔm 'vɛm]
About what?	Om hva?	[ɔm 'va]
With whom?	Med hvem?	[me 'vɛm]
How many?	Hvor mange?	[vʉr 'maŋe]
How much?	Hvor mye?	[vʉr 'mye]
Whose?	Hvis?	['vis]

4. Prepositions

with (accompanied by)	med	[me]
without	uten	['ʉtən]
to (indicating direction)	til	['til]
about (talking ~ ...)	om	['ɔm]
before (in time)	før	['før]
in front of ...	foran, framfor	['fɔran], ['framfɔr]
under (beneath, below)	under	['ʉnər]
above (over)	over	['ɔvər]
on (atop)	på	['pɔ]
from (off, out of)	fra	['fra]
of (made from)	av	[ɑ:]
in (e.g. ~ ten minutes)	om	['ɔm]
over (across the top of)	over	['ɔvər]

5. Function words. Adverbs. Part 1

Where? (at, in)	Hvor?	['vʊr]
here (adv)	her	['hɛr]
there (adv)	der	['dɛr]
somewhere (to be)	et sted	[et 'sted]
nowhere (not anywhere)	ingensteds	['iŋən‚stɛts]
by (near, beside)	ved	['ve]
by the window	ved vinduet	[ve 'vindʉə]
Where (to)?	Hvorhen?	['vʊrhen]
here (e.g. come ~!)	hit	['hit]
there (e.g. to go ~)	dit	['dit]
from here (adv)	herfra	['hɛr‚fra]
from there (adv)	derfra	['dɛr‚fra]
close (adv)	nær	['nær]
far (adv)	langt	['laŋt]
near (e.g. ~ Paris)	nær	['nær]
nearby (adv)	i nærheten	[i 'nær‚hetən]
not far (adv)	ikke langt	['ikə 'laŋt]
left (adj)	venstre	['vɛnstrə]
on the left	til venstre	[til 'vɛnstrə]
to the left	til venstre	[til 'vɛnstrə]
right (adj)	høyre	['højrə]
on the right	til høyre	[til 'højrə]
to the right	til høyre	[til 'højrə]
in front (adv)	foran	['foran]
front (as adj)	fremre	['frɛmrə]
ahead (the kids ran ~)	fram	['fram]
behind (adv)	bakom	['bakɔm]
from behind	bakfra	['bak‚fra]
back (towards the rear)	tilbake	[til'bakə]
middle	midt (m)	['mit]
in the middle	i midten	[i 'mitən]
at the side	fra siden	[fra 'sidən]
everywhere (adv)	overalt	[ɔvər'alt]
around (in all directions)	rundt omkring	['rʉnt ɔm'kriŋ]
from inside	innefra	['inə‚fra]
somewhere (to go)	et sted	[et 'sted]
straight (directly)	rett, direkte	['rɛt], ['di'rɛktə]
back (e.g. come ~)	tilbake	[til'bakə]
from anywhere	et eller annet steds fra	[et 'elər ‚aːnt 'stɛts fra]
from somewhere	et eller annet steds fra	[et 'elər ‚aːnt 'stɛts fra]

firstly (adv)	for det første	[fɔr de 'fœʂtə]
secondly (adv)	for det annet	[fɔr de 'ɑːnt]
thirdly (adv)	for det tredje	[fɔr de 'trɛdje]

suddenly (adv)	plutselig	['plʉtseli]
at first (in the beginning)	i begynnelsen	[i be'jinəlsən]
for the first time	for første gang	[fɔr 'fœʂtə ˌgɑŋ]
long before ...	lenge før ...	['leŋə 'før ...]
anew (over again)	på nytt	[pɔ 'nʏt]
for good (adv)	for godt	[fɔr 'gɔt]

never (adv)	aldri	['ɑldri]
again (adv)	igjen	[i'jɛn]
now (adv)	nå	['nɔ]
often (adv)	ofte	['ɔftə]
then (adv)	da	['dɑ]
urgently (quickly)	omgående	['ɔmˌgɔːnə]
usually (adv)	vanligvis	['vɑnliˌvis]

by the way, ...	forresten, ...	[fɔ'rɛstən ...]
possible (that is ~)	mulig, kanskje	['mʉli], ['kanʂə]
probably (adv)	sannsynligvis	[san'sʏnliˌvis]
maybe (adv)	kanskje	['kanʂə]
besides ...	dessuten, ...	[des'ʉtən ...]
that's why ...	derfor ...	['dɛrfɔr ...]
in spite of ...	på tross av ...	['pɔ 'trɔs ɑː ...]
thanks to ...	takket være ...	['tɑkət ˌværə ...]

what (pron.)	hva	['vɑ]
that (conj.)	at	[ɑt]
something	noe	['nʊe]
anything (something)	noe	['nʊe]
nothing	ingenting	['iŋəntiŋ]

who (pron.)	hvem	['vɛm]
someone	noen	['nʊən]
somebody	noen	['nʊən]

nobody	ingen	['iŋən]
nowhere (a voyage to ~)	ingensteds	['iŋənˌstɛts]
nobody's	ingens	['iŋəns]
somebody's	noens	['nʊəns]

so (I'm ~ glad)	så	['sɔː]
also (as well)	også	['ɔsɔ]
too (as well)	også	['ɔsɔ]

6. Function words. Adverbs. Part 2

Why?	Hvorfor?	['vʊrfʊr]
for some reason	av en eller annen grunn	[ɑː en elər 'ɑnən ˌgrʉn]
because ...	fordi ...	[fɔ'di ...]
for some purpose	av en eller annen grunn	[ɑː en elər 'ɑnən ˌgrʉn]
and	og	['ɔ]

or	eller	['elər]
but	men	['men]
for (e.g. ~ me)	for, til	[fɔr], [til]

too (excessively)	for, altfor	['fɔr], ['altfor]
only (exclusively)	bare	['barə]
exactly (adv)	presis, eksakt	[prɛ'sis], [ɛk'sɑkt]
about (more or less)	cirka	['sirkɑ]

approximately (adv)	omtrent	[ɔm'trɛnt]
approximate (adj)	omtrentlig	[ɔm'trɛntli]
almost (adv)	nesten	['nɛstən]
the rest	rest (m)	['rɛst]

the other (second)	den annen	[den 'anən]
other (different)	andre	['andrə]
each (adj)	hver	['vɛr]
any (no matter which)	hvilken som helst	['vilkən sɔm 'hɛlst]
many, much (a lot of)	mye	['mye]
many people	mange	['maŋə]
all (everyone)	alle	['alə]

in return for ...	til gjengjeld for ...	[til 'jɛnjɛl for ...]
in exchange (adv)	istedenfor	[i'steden,for]
by hand (made)	for hånd	[for 'hɔn]
hardly (negative opinion)	neppe	['nepə]

probably (adv)	sannsynligvis	[san'synli,vis]
on purpose (intentionally)	med vilje	[me 'viljə]
by accident (adv)	tilfeldigvis	[til'fɛldivis]

very (adv)	meget	['meget]
for example (adv)	for eksempel	[for ɛk'sɛmpəl]
between	mellom	['mɛlom]
among	blant	['blant]
so much (such a lot)	så mye	['sɔ: mye]
especially (adv)	særlig	['sæ:ḷi]

NUMBERS. MISCELLANEOUS

7. Cardinal numbers. Part 1

0 zero	null	['nʉl]
1 one	en	['en]
2 two	to	['tʊ]
3 three	tre	['tre]
4 four	fire	['fire]
5 five	fem	['fɛm]
6 six	seks	['sɛks]
7 seven	sju	['ʂʉ]
8 eight	åtte	['ɔtə]
9 nine	ni	['ni]
10 ten	ti	['ti]
11 eleven	elleve	['ɛlvə]
12 twelve	tolv	['tɔl]
13 thirteen	tretten	['trɛtən]
14 fourteen	fjorten	['fjɔ:ʈən]
15 fifteen	femten	['fɛmtən]
16 sixteen	seksten	['sæjstən]
17 seventeen	sytten	['sʏtən]
18 eighteen	atten	['atən]
19 nineteen	nitten	['nitən]
20 twenty	tjue	['çʉe]
21 twenty-one	tjueen	['çʉe en]
22 twenty-two	tjueto	['çʉe tʊ]
23 twenty-three	tjuetre	['çʉe tre]
30 thirty	tretti	['trɛti]
31 thirty-one	trettien	['trɛti en]
32 thirty-two	trettito	['trɛti tʊ]
33 thirty-three	trettitre	['trɛti tre]
40 forty	førti	['fœ:ʈi]
41 forty-one	førtien	['fœ:ʈi en]
42 forty-two	førtito	['fœ:ʈi tʊ]
43 forty-three	førtitre	['fœ:ʈi tre]
50 fifty	femti	['fɛmti]
51 fifty-one	femtien	['fɛmti en]
52 fifty-two	femtito	['fɛmti tʊ]
53 fifty-three	femtitre	['fɛmti tre]
60 sixty	seksti	['sɛksti]
61 sixty-one	sekstien	['sɛksti en]

| 62 sixty-two | sekstito | ['sɛksti tʉ] |
| 63 sixty-three | sekstitre | ['sɛksti tre] |

70 seventy	sytti	['sʏti]
71 seventy-one	syttien	['sʏti en]
72 seventy-two	syttito	['sʏti tʉ]
73 seventy-three	syttitre	['sʏti tre]

80 eighty	åtti	['ɔti]
81 eighty-one	åttien	['ɔti en]
82 eighty-two	åttito	['ɔti tʉ]
83 eighty-three	åttitre	['ɔti tre]

90 ninety	nitti	['niti]
91 ninety-one	nittien	['niti en]
92 ninety-two	nittito	['niti tʉ]
93 ninety-three	nittitre	['niti tre]

8. Cardinal numbers. Part 2

100 one hundred	hundre	['hʉndrə]
200 two hundred	to hundre	['tʉ ˌhʉndrə]
300 three hundred	tre hundre	['tre ˌhʉndrə]
400 four hundred	fire hundre	['fire ˌhʉndrə]
500 five hundred	fem hundre	['fɛm ˌhʉndrə]

600 six hundred	seks hundre	['sɛks ˌhʉndrə]
700 seven hundred	syv hundre	['syv ˌhʉndrə]
800 eight hundred	åtte hundre	['ɔtə ˌhʉndrə]
900 nine hundred	ni hundre	['ni ˌhʉndrə]

1000 one thousand	tusen	['tʉsən]
2000 two thousand	to tusen	['tʉ ˌtʉsən]
3000 three thousand	tre tusen	['tre ˌtʉsən]
10000 ten thousand	ti tusen	['ti ˌtʉsən]
one hundred thousand	hundre tusen	['hʉndrə ˌtʉsən]
million	million (m)	[mi'ljun]
billion	milliard (m)	[mi'lja:ɖ]

9. Ordinal numbers

first (adj)	første	['fœʂtə]
second (adj)	annen	['ɑnən]
third (adj)	tredje	['trɛdjə]
fourth (adj)	fjerde	['fjærə]
fifth (adj)	femte	['fɛmtə]

sixth (adj)	sjette	['ʂɛtə]
seventh (adj)	sjuende	['ʂʉenə]
eighth (adj)	åttende	['ɔtenə]
ninth (adj)	niende	['nienə]
tenth (adj)	tiende	['tienə]

COLORS. UNITS OF MEASUREMENT

10. Colours

colour	farge (m)	['fargə]
shade (tint)	nyanse (m)	[ny'anse]
hue	fargetone (m)	['fargə‚tunə]
rainbow	regnbue (m)	['ræjn‚bɥːə]
white (adj)	hvit	['vit]
black (adj)	svart	['svɑːt̪]
grey (adj)	grå	['grɔ]
green (adj)	grønn	['grœn]
yellow (adj)	gul	['gɥl]
red (adj)	rød	['rø]
blue (adj)	blå	['blɔ]
light blue (adj)	lyseblå	['lysə‚blɔ]
pink (adj)	rosa	['rosa]
orange (adj)	oransje	[ɔ'ranʂɛ]
violet (adj)	fiolett	[fiʊ'lət]
brown (adj)	brun	['brɥn]
golden (adj)	gullgul	['gɥl]
silvery (adj)	sølv-	['søl-]
beige (adj)	beige	['bɛːʂ]
cream (adj)	kr{e/œ}mfarget	['krɛm‚farget]
turquoise (adj)	turkis	[tʉr'kis]
cherry red (adj)	kirsebærrød	['çɪʂəbær‚rød]
lilac (adj)	lilla	['lila]
crimson (adj)	karminrød	['karmʊ'sin‚rød]
light (adj)	lys	['lys]
dark (adj)	mørk	['mœrk]
bright, vivid (adj)	klar	['klar]
coloured (pencils)	farge-	['fargə-]
colour (e.g. ~ film)	farge-	['fargə-]
black-and-white (adj)	svart-hvit	['svɑːt̪ vit]
plain (one-coloured)	ensfarget	['ɛns‚farget]
multicoloured (adj)	mangefarget	['maŋə‚farget]

11. Units of measurement

weight	vekt (m)	['vɛkt]
length	lengde (m/f)	['leŋdə]

width	bredde (m)	['brɛdə]
height	høyde (m)	['højdə]
depth	dybde (m)	['dʏbdə]
volume	volum (n)	[vɔ'lʉm]
area	areal (n)	[ˌare'al]

gram	gram (n)	['gram]
milligram	milligram (n)	['miliˌgram]
kilogram	kilogram (n)	['çiluˌgram]
ton	tonn (m/n)	['tɔn]
pound	pund (n)	['pʉn]
ounce	unse (m)	['ʉnsə]

metre	meter (m)	['metər]
millimetre	millimeter (m)	['miliˌmetər]
centimetre	centimeter (m)	['sɛntiˌmetər]
kilometre	kilometer (m)	['çiluˌmetər]
mile	mil (m/f)	['mil]

inch	tomme (m)	['tɔmə]
foot	fot (m)	['fʊt]
yard	yard (m)	['ja:rd]

| square metre | kvadratmeter (m) | [kva'dratˌmetər] |
| hectare | hektar (n) | ['hɛktar] |

litre	liter (m)	['litər]
degree	grad (m)	['grad]
volt	volt (m)	['vɔlt]
ampere	ampere (m)	[am'pɛr]
horsepower	hestekraft (m/f)	['hɛstəˌkraft]

quantity	mengde (m)	['mɛŋdə]
a little bit of …	få …	['fɔ …]
half	halvdel (m)	['haldel]
dozen	dusin (n)	[dʉ'sin]
piece (item)	stykke (n)	['stʏkə]

| size | størrelse (m) | ['stœrəlsə] |
| scale (map ~) | målestokk (m) | ['mo:ləˌstɔk] |

minimal (adj)	minimal	[mini'mal]
the smallest (adj)	minste	['minstə]
medium (adj)	middel-	['midəl-]
maximal (adj)	maksimal	[maksi'mal]
the largest (adj)	største	['stœҫstə]

12. Containers

canning jar (glass ~)	glaskrukke (m/f)	['glasˌkrʉkə]
tin, can	boks (m)	['bɔks]
bucket	bøtte (m/f)	['bœtə]
barrel	tønne (m)	['tœnə]
wash basin (e.g., plastic ~)	vaskefat (n)	['vaskəˌfat]

tank (100L water ~)	tank (m)	['taŋk]
hip flask	lommelerke (m/f)	['lʊmə‚lærkə]
jerrycan	bensinkanne (m/f)	[bɛn'sin‚kanə]
tank (e.g., tank car)	tank (m)	['taŋk]
mug	krus (n)	['krʉs]
cup (of coffee, etc.)	kopp (m)	['kɔp]
saucer	tefat (n)	['te‚fat]
glass (tumbler)	glass (n)	['glas]
wine glass	vinglass (n)	['vin‚glas]
stock pot (soup pot)	gryte (m/f)	['grytə]
bottle (~ of wine)	flaske (m)	['flaskə]
neck (of the bottle, etc.)	flaskehals (m)	['flaskə‚hals]
carafe (decanter)	karaffel (m)	[ka'rafəl]
pitcher	mugge (m/f)	['mʉgə]
vessel (container)	beholder (m)	[be'hɔlər]
pot (crock, stoneware ~)	pott, potte (m)	['pɔt], ['potə]
vase	vase (m)	['vasə]
bottle (perfume ~)	flakong (m)	[fla'kɔŋ]
vial, small bottle	flaske (m/f)	['flaskə]
tube (of toothpaste)	tube (m)	['tʉbə]
sack (bag)	sekk (m)	['sɛk]
bag (paper ~, plastic ~)	pose (m)	['pʉsə]
packet (of cigarettes, etc.)	pakke (m/f)	['pakə]
box (e.g. shoebox)	eske (m/f)	['ɛskə]
crate	kasse (m/f)	['kasə]
basket	kurv (m)	['kʉrv]

MAIN VERBS

13. The most important verbs. Part 1

to advise (vt)	å råde	[ɔ 'roːdə]
to agree (say yes)	å samtykke	[ɔ 'sɑmˌtʏkə]
to answer (vi, vt)	å svare	[ɔ 'svɑrə]
to apologize (vi)	å unnskylde seg	[ɔ 'ʉnˌʂʏlə sæj]
to arrive (vi)	å ankomme	[ɔ 'ɑnˌkɔmə]
to ask (~ oneself)	å spørre	[ɔ 'spørə]
to ask (~ sb to do sth)	å be	[ɔ 'be]
to be (vi)	å være	[ɔ 'værə]
to be afraid	å frykte	[ɔ 'frʏktə]
to be hungry	å være sulten	[ɔ 'værə 'sʉltən]
to be interested in ...	å interessere seg	[ɔ intəre'serə sæj]
to be needed	å være behøv	[ɔ 'værə be'høv]
to be surprised	å bli forundret	[ɔ 'bli fɔ'rʉndrət]
to be thirsty	å være tørst	[ɔ 'værə 'tœʂt]
to begin (vt)	å begynne	[ɔ be'jinə]
to belong to ...	å tilhøre ...	[ɔ 'tilˌhørə ...]
to boast (vi)	å prale	[ɔ 'prɑlə]
to break (split into pieces)	å bryte	[ɔ 'brytə]
to call (~ for help)	å tilkalle	[ɔ 'tilˌkɑlə]
can (v aux)	å kunne	[ɔ 'kʉnə]
to catch (vt)	å fange	[ɔ 'fɑŋə]
to change (vt)	å endre	[ɔ 'ɛndrə]
to choose (select)	å velge	[ɔ 'vɛlgə]
to come down (the stairs)	å gå ned	[ɔ 'gɔ ne]
to compare (vt)	å sammenlikne	[ɔ 'sɑmənˌliknə]
to complain (vi, vt)	å klage	[ɔ 'klɑgə]
to confuse (mix up)	å forveksle	[ɔ fɔr'vɛkʂlə]
to continue (vt)	å fortsette	[ɔ 'fortˌsɛtə]
to control (vt)	å kontrollere	[ɔ kʉntrɔ'lerə]
to cook (dinner)	å lage	[ɔ 'lɑgə]
to cost (vt)	å koste	[ɔ 'kɔstə]
to count (add up)	å telle	[ɔ 'tɛlə]
to count on ...	å regne med ...	[ɔ 'rɛjnə me ...]
to create (vt)	å opprette	[ɔ 'ɔpˌrɛtə]
to cry (weep)	å gråte	[ɔ 'groːtə]

14. The most important verbs. Part 2

to deceive (vi, vt)	å fuske	[ɔ 'fʉskə]
to decorate (tree, street)	å pryde	[ɔ 'prydə]

to defend (a country, etc.)	å forsvare	[ɔ fɔ'ṣvɑrə]
to demand (request firmly)	å kreve	[ɔ 'krevə]
to dig (vt)	å grave	[ɔ 'grɑvə]

to discuss (vt)	å diskutere	[ɔ disku'terə]
to do (vt)	å gjøre	[ɔ 'jørə]
to doubt (have doubts)	å tvile	[ɔ 'tvilə]
to drop (let fall)	å tappe	[ɔ 'tɑpə]
to enter (room, house, etc.)	å komme inn	[ɔ 'kɔmə in]

to excuse (forgive)	å unnskylde	[ɔ 'un̩ṣylə]
to exist (vi)	å eksistere	[ɔ ɛksi'sterə]
to expect (foresee)	å forutse	[ɔ 'fɔrut̩sə]
to explain (vt)	å forklare	[ɔ fɔr'klɑrə]
to fall (vi)	å falle	[ɔ 'fɑlə]

to fancy (vt)	å like	[ɔ 'likə]
to find (vt)	å finne	[ɔ 'finə]
to finish (vt)	å slutte	[ɔ 'ṣlutə]
to fly (vi)	å fly	[ɔ 'fly]
to follow ... (come after)	å følge etter ...	[ɔ 'følə 'ɛtər ...]

to forget (vi, vt)	å glemme	[ɔ 'glemə]
to forgive (vt)	å tilgi	[ɔ 'til̩ji]
to give (vt)	å gi	[ɔ 'ji]
to give a hint	å gi et vink	[ɔ 'ji et 'vink]
to go (on foot)	å gå	[ɔ 'gɔ]

to go for a swim	å bade	[ɔ 'bɑdə]
to go out (for dinner, etc.)	å gå ut	[ɔ 'gɔ ut]
to guess (the answer)	å gjette	[ɔ 'jɛtə]

to have (vt)	å ha	[ɔ 'hɑ]
to have breakfast	å spise frokost	[ɔ 'spisə ˌfrukɔst]
to have dinner	å spise middag	[ɔ 'spisə 'mi̩dɑ]
to have lunch	å spise lunsj	[ɔ 'spisə ˌlunṣ]
to hear (vt)	å høre	[ɔ 'hørə]

to help (vt)	å hjelpe	[ɔ 'jɛlpə]
to hide (vt)	å gjemme	[ɔ 'jɛmə]
to hope (vi, vt)	å håpe	[ɔ 'ho:pə]
to hunt (vi, vt)	å jage	[ɔ 'jɑgə]
to hurry (vi)	å skynde seg	[ɔ 'ṣynə sæj]

15. The most important verbs. Part 3

to inform (vt)	å informere	[ɔ infɔr'merə]
to insist (vi, vt)	å insistere	[ɔ insi'sterə]
to insult (vt)	å fornærme	[ɔ fɔ:'n̩ærmə]
to invite (vt)	å innby, å invitere	[ɔ 'inby], [ɔ invi'terə]
to joke (vi)	å spøke	[ɔ 'spøkə]

| to keep (vt) | å beholde | [ɔ be'hɔlə] |
| to keep silent | å tie | [ɔ 'tie] |

to kill (vt)	å døde, å myrde	[ɔ 'dødə], [ɔ 'mʏːdə]
to know (sb)	å kjenne	[ɔ 'çɛnə]
to know (sth)	å vite	[ɔ 'vitə]
to laugh (vi)	å le, å skratte	[ɔ 'le], [ɔ 'skratə]

to liberate (city, etc.)	å befri	[ɔ beˈfri]
to look for ... (search)	å søke ...	[ɔ 'søkə ...]
to love (sb)	å elske	[ɔ 'ɛlskə]
to make a mistake	å gjøre feil	[ɔ 'jørə ˌfæjl]
to manage, to run	å styre, å lede	[ɔ 'styrə], [ɔ 'ledə]

to mean (signify)	å bety	[ɔ 'bety]
to mention (talk about)	å omtale, å nevne	[ɔ 'ɔmˌtalə], [ɔ 'nɛvnə]
to miss (school, etc.)	å skulke	[ɔ 'skʉlkə]
to notice (see)	å bemerke	[ɔ beˈmærkə]
to object (vi, vt)	å innvende	[ɔ 'inˌvɛnə]

to observe (see)	å observere	[ɔ ɔbsɛrˈverə]
to open (vt)	å åpne	[ɔ 'ɔpnə]
to order (meal, etc.)	å bestille	[ɔ beˈstilə]
to order (mil.)	å beordre	[ɔ beˈɔrdrə]
to own (possess)	å besidde, å eie	[ɔ bɛˈsidə], [ɔ 'æjə]

to participate (vi)	å delta	[ɔ 'dɛlta]
to pay (vi, vt)	å betale	[ɔ beˈtalə]
to permit (vt)	å tillate	[ɔ 'tiˌlatə]
to plan (vt)	å planlegge	[ɔ 'planˌlegə]
to play (children)	å leke	[ɔ 'lekə]

to pray (vi, vt)	å be	[ɔ 'be]
to prefer (vt)	å foretrekke	[ɔ 'forɛˌtrɛkə]
to promise (vt)	å love	[ɔ 'lɔvə]
to pronounce (vt)	å uttale	[ɔ 'ʉtˌtalə]
to propose (vt)	å foreslå	[ɔ 'forɛˌʂlɔ]
to punish (vt)	å straffe	[ɔ 'strafə]

16. The most important verbs. Part 4

to read (vi, vt)	å lese	[ɔ 'lesə]
to recommend (vt)	å anbefale	[ɔ 'anbeˌfalə]
to refuse (vi, vt)	å vegre seg	[ɔ 'vɛgrə sæj]
to regret (be sorry)	å beklage	[ɔ beˈklagə]
to rent (sth from sb)	å leie	[ɔ 'læjə]

to repeat (say again)	å gjenta	[ɔ 'jɛnta]
to reserve, to book	å reservere	[ɔ resɛrˈverə]
to run (vi)	å løpe	[ɔ 'løpə]
to save (rescue)	å redde	[ɔ 'rɛdə]

to say (~ thank you)	å si	[ɔ 'si]
to scold (vt)	å skjelle	[ɔ 'ʂɛːlə]
to see (vt)	å se	[ɔ 'se]
to sell (vt)	å selge	[ɔ 'sɛlə]
to send (vt)	å sende	[ɔ 'sɛnə]

to shoot (vi)	å skyte	[ɔ 'ʂytə]
to shout (vi)	å skrike	[ɔ 'skrikə]
to show (vt)	å vise	[ɔ 'visə]
to sign (document)	å underskrive	[ɔ 'ʉnəˌʂkrivə]

to sit down (vi)	å sette seg	[ɔ 'sɛtə sæj]
to smile (vi)	å smile	[ɔ 'smilə]
to speak (vi, vt)	å tale	[ɔ 'talə]
to steal (money, etc.)	å stjele	[ɔ 'stjelə]
to stop (for pause, etc.)	å stoppe	[ɔ 'stɔpə]

to stop (please ~ calling me)	å slutte	[ɔ 'ʂlʉtə]
to study (vt)	å studere	[ɔ stʉ'derə]
to swim (vi)	å svømme	[ɔ 'svœmə]
to take (vt)	å ta	[ɔ 'ta]
to think (vi, vt)	å tenke	[ɔ 'tɛnkə]

to threaten (vt)	å true	[ɔ 'trʉə]
to touch (with hands)	å røre	[ɔ 'rørə]
to translate (vt)	å oversette	[ɔ 'ɔvəˌsɛtə]
to trust (vt)	å stole på	[ɔ 'stʉlə pɔ]
to try (attempt)	å prøve	[ɔ 'prøvə]

to turn (e.g., ~ left)	å svinge	[ɔ 'sviŋə]
to underestimate (vt)	å undervurdere	[ɔ 'ʉnərvu:ˌderə]
to understand (vt)	å forstå	[ɔ fɔ'ʂtɔ]
to unite (vt)	å forene	[ɔ fɔ'renə]
to wait (vt)	å vente	[ɔ 'vɛntə]

to want (wish, desire)	å ville	[ɔ 'vilə]
to warn (vt)	å varsle	[ɔ 'vaʂlə]
to work (vi)	å arbeide	[ɔ 'arˌbæjdə]
to write (vt)	å skrive	[ɔ 'skrivə]
to write down	å skrive ned	[ɔ 'skrivə ne]

TIME. CALENDAR

17. Weekdays

Monday	mandag (m)	['mɑn‚dɑ]
Tuesday	tirsdag (m)	['tiʂ‚dɑ]
Wednesday	onsdag (m)	['ʉns‚dɑ]
Thursday	torsdag (m)	['toʂ‚dɑ]
Friday	fredag (m)	['frɛ‚dɑ]
Saturday	lørdag (m)	['lør‚dɑ]
Sunday	søndag (m)	['søn‚dɑ]
today (adv)	i dag	[i 'dɑ]
tomorrow (adv)	i morgen	[i 'mɔːən]
the day after tomorrow	i overmorgen	[i 'ɔvər‚mɔːən]
yesterday (adv)	i går	[i 'gɔr]
the day before yesterday	i forgårs	[i 'fɔr‚gɔʂ]
day	dag (m)	['dɑ]
working day	arbeidsdag (m)	['ɑrbæjds‚dɑ]
public holiday	festdag (m)	['fɛst‚dɑ]
day off	fridag (m)	['fri‚dɑ]
weekend	ukeslutt (m), helg (f)	['ʉkə‚ʂlʉt], ['hɛlg]
all day long	hele dagen	['helə 'dɑgən]
the next day (adv)	neste dag	['nɛstə ‚dɑ]
two days ago	for to dager siden	[fɔr tʉ 'dɑgər ‚sidən]
the day before	dagen før	['dɑgən 'før]
daily (adj)	daglig	['dɑgli]
every day (adv)	hver dag	['vɛr dɑ]
week	uke (m/f)	['ʉkə]
last week (adv)	siste uke	['sistə 'ʉkə]
next week (adv)	i neste uke	[i 'nɛstə 'ʉkə]
weekly (adj)	ukentlig	['ʉkəntli]
every week (adv)	hver uke	['vɛr 'ʉkə]
twice a week	to ganger per uke	['tʉ 'gɑŋər per 'ʉkə]
every Tuesday	hver tirsdag	['vɛr 'tiʂdɑ]

18. Hours. Day and night

morning	morgen (m)	['mɔːən]
in the morning	om morgenen	[ɔm 'mɔːenən]
noon, midday	middag (m)	['mi‚dɑ]
in the afternoon	om ettermiddagen	[ɔm 'ɛtər‚midɑgən]
evening	kveld (m)	['kvɛl]
in the evening	om kvelden	[ɔm 'kvɛlən]

night	natt (m/f)	['nɑt]
at night	om natta	[ɔm 'nɑtɑ]
midnight	midnatt (m/f)	['mid.nɑt]

second	sekund (m/n)	[se'kʉn]
minute	minutt (n)	[mi'nʉt]
hour	time (m)	['timə]
half an hour	halvtime (m)	['hɑl.timə]
a quarter-hour	kvarter (n)	[kvɑ:ʈer]
fifteen minutes	femten minutter	['fɛmtən mi'nʉtər]
24 hours	døgn (n)	['døjn]

sunrise	soloppgang (m)	['sʉlɔp.gɑŋ]
dawn	daggry (n)	['dɑg.gry]
early morning	tidlig morgen (m)	['tili 'mɔ:ən]
sunset	solnedgang (m)	['sʉlned.gɑŋ]

early in the morning	tidlig om morgenen	['tili ɔm 'mɔ:enən]
this morning	i morges	[i 'mɔrəs]
tomorrow morning	i morgen tidlig	[i 'mɔ:ən 'tili]

this afternoon	i formiddag	[i 'fɔrmi.dɑ]
in the afternoon	om ettermiddagen	[ɔm 'ɛtər.midɑgən]
tomorrow afternoon	i morgen ettermiddag	[i 'mɔ:ən 'ɛtər.midɑ]

| tonight (this evening) | i kveld | [i 'kvɛl] |
| tomorrow night | i morgen kveld | [i 'mɔ:ən ˌkvɛl] |

at 3 o'clock sharp	presis klokka tre	[prɛ'sis 'klɔkɑ tre]
about 4 o'clock	ved fire-tiden	[ve 'fire ˌtidən]
by 12 o'clock	innen klokken tolv	['inən 'klɔkən tɔl]

in 20 minutes	om tjue minutter	[ɔm 'çʉə mi'nʉtər]
in an hour	om en time	[ɔm en 'timə]
on time (adv)	i tide	[i 'tidə]

a quarter to ...	kvart på ...	['kvɑ:ʈ pɔ ...]
within an hour	innen en time	['inən en 'time]
every 15 minutes	hvert kvarter	['vɛ:ʈ kvɑ:'ʈer]
round the clock	døgnet rundt	['døjne ˌrʉnt]

19. Months. Seasons

January	januar (m)	['jɑnʉˌɑr]
February	februar (m)	['febrʉˌɑr]
March	mars (m)	['mɑʂ]
April	april (m)	[ɑ'pril]
May	mai (m)	['mɑj]
June	juni (m)	['jʉni]

July	juli (m)	['jʉli]
August	august (m)	[aʉ'gʉst]
September	september (m)	[sep'tɛmbər]
October	oktober (m)	[ɔk'tʉbər]

November	november (m)	[nʊ'vɛmbər]
December	desember (m)	[de'sɛmbər]

spring	vår (m)	['vɔːr]
in spring	om våren	[ɔm 'voːrən]
spring (as adj)	vår-, vårlig	['vɔːr-], ['vɔːli]

summer	sommer (m)	['sɔmər]
in summer	om sommeren	[ɔm 'sɔmerən]
summer (as adj)	sommer-	['sɔmər-]

autumn	høst (m)	['høst]
in autumn	om høsten	[ɔm 'høstən]
autumn (as adj)	høst-, høstlig	['høst-], ['høstli]

winter	vinter (m)	['vintər]
in winter	om vinteren	[ɔm 'vinterən]
winter (as adj)	vinter-	['vintər-]

month	måned (m)	['moːnət]
this month	denne måneden	['dɛnə 'moːnedən]
next month	neste måned	['nɛstə 'moːnət]
last month	forrige måned	['foriə ˌmoːnət]

a month ago	for en måned siden	[fɔr en 'moːnət ˌsidən]
in a month (a month later)	om en måned	[ɔm en 'moːnət]
in 2 months (2 months later)	om to måneder	[ɔm 'tʊ 'moːnedər]
the whole month	en hel måned	[en 'hel 'moːnət]
all month long	hele måned	['helə 'moːnət]

monthly (~ magazine)	månedlig	['moːnədli]
monthly (adv)	månedligt	['moːnedlət]
every month	hver måned	[ˌvɛr 'moːnət]
twice a month	to ganger per måned	['tʊ 'gaŋər per 'moːnət]

year	år (n)	['ɔr]
this year	i år	[i 'oːr]
next year	neste år	['nɛstə ˌoːr]
last year	i fjor	[i 'fjɔr]

a year ago	for et år siden	[fɔr et 'oːr ˌsidən]
in a year	om et år	[ɔm et 'oːr]
in two years	om to år	[ɔm 'tʊ 'oːr]
the whole year	hele året	['helə 'oːre]
all year long	hele året	['helə 'oːre]

every year	hvert år	['vɛːʈ 'oːr]
annual (adj)	årlig	['oːli]
annually (adv)	årlig, hvert år	['oːli], ['vɛːʈ 'ɔr]
4 times a year	fire ganger per år	['fire 'gaŋər per 'oːr]

date (e.g. today's ~)	dato (m)	['datʊ]
date (e.g. ~ of birth)	dato (m)	['datʊ]
calendar	kalender (m)	[ka'lendər]
half a year	halvår (n)	['halˌoːr]
six months	halvår (n)	['halˌoːr]

| season (summer, etc.) | **årstid** (m/f) | [ˈoːʂˌtid] |
| century | **århundre** (n) | [ˈɔrˌhʉndrə] |

TRAVEL. HOTEL

20. Trip. Travel

tourism, travel	turisme (m)	[tʉ'rismə]
tourist	turist (m)	[tʉ'rist]
trip, voyage	reise (m/f)	['ræjsə]
adventure	eventyr (n)	['ɛvən‚tyr]
trip, journey	tripp (m)	['trip]
holiday	ferie (m)	['fɛriə]
to be on holiday	å være på ferie	[ɔ 'værə pɔ 'fɛriə]
rest	hvile (m/f)	['vilə]
train	tog (n)	['tɔg]
by train	med tog	[me 'tɔg]
aeroplane	fly (n)	['fly]
by aeroplane	med fly	[me 'fly]
by car	med bil	[me 'bil]
by ship	med skip	[me 'şip]
luggage	bagasje (m)	[ba'gaşə]
suitcase	koffert (m)	['kʉfɛ:t]
luggage trolley	bagasjetralle (m/f)	[ba'gaşə‚tralə]
passport	pass (n)	['pas]
visa	visum (n)	['visʉm]
ticket	billett (m)	[bi'let]
air ticket	flybillett (m)	['fly bi'let]
guidebook	reisehåndbok (m/f)	['ræjsə‚hɔnbʉk]
map (tourist ~)	kart (n)	['ka:t]
area (rural ~)	område (n)	['ɔm‚ro:də]
place, site	sted (n)	['sted]
exotic (adj)	eksotisk	[ɛk'sʉtisk]
amazing (adj)	forunderlig	[fo'rʉnde:[i]
group	gruppe (m)	['grʉpə]
excursion, sightseeing tour	utflukt (m/f)	['ʉt‚flʉkt]
guide (person)	guide (m)	['gajd]

21. Hotel

hotel	hotell (n)	[hʉ'tɛl]
motel	motell (n)	[mʉ'tɛl]
three-star (~ hotel)	trestjernet	['tre‚stjæ:ŋə]
five-star	femstjernet	['fɛm‚stjæ:ŋə]

to stay (in a hotel, etc.)	å bo	[ɔ 'bʊ]
room	rom (n)	['rʊm]
single room	enkeltrom (n)	['ɛnkelt,rʊm]
double room	dobbeltrom (n)	['dɔbəlt,rʊm]
to book a room	å reservere rom	[ɔ resɛr'verə 'rʊm]

| half board | halvpensjon (m) | ['hal pan,sʊn] |
| full board | fullpensjon (m) | ['fʉl pan,sʊn] |

with bath	med badekar	[me 'badə,kar]
with shower	med dusj	[me 'dʉʃ]
satellite television	satellitt-TV (m)	[satɛ'lit 'tɛvɛ]
air-conditioner	klimaanlegg (n)	['klima'an,leg]
towel	håndkle (n)	['hɔn,kle]
key	nøkkel (m)	['nøkəl]

administrator	administrator (m)	[admini'strɑːtʊr]
chambermaid	stuepike (m/f)	['stʉə,pikə]
porter	pikkolo (m)	['pikɔlɔ]
doorman	portier (m)	[pɔ:'tje]

restaurant	restaurant (m)	[rɛstʊ'raŋ]
pub, bar	bar (m)	['bar]
breakfast	frokost (m)	['frʊkɔst]
dinner	middag (m)	['mi,da]
buffet	buffet (m)	[bʉ'fɛ]

| lobby | hall, lobby (m) | ['hal], ['lɔbi] |
| lift | heis (m) | ['hæjs] |

| DO NOT DISTURB | VENNLIGST IKKE FORSTYRR! | ['vɛnligt ikə fɔ'ʂtyr] |
| NO SMOKING | RØYKING FORBUDT | ['røjkiŋ fɔr'bʉt] |

22. Sightseeing

monument	monument (n)	[mɔnʉ'mɛnt]
fortress	festning (m/f)	['fɛstniŋ]
palace	palass (n)	[pa'las]
castle	borg (m)	['bɔrg]
tower	tårn (n)	['tɔːŋ]
mausoleum	mausoleum (n)	[maʊsʊ'leum]

architecture	arkitektur (m)	[arkitɛk'tʉr]
medieval (adj)	middelalderlig	['midəl,aldɛː[i]
ancient (adj)	gammel	['gaməl]
national (adj)	nasjonal	[naʂʊ'nal]
famous (monument, etc.)	kjent	['çɛnt]

tourist	turist (m)	[tʉ'rist]
guide (person)	guide (m)	['gajd]
excursion, sightseeing tour	utflukt (m/f)	['ʉt,flʉkt]
to show (vt)	å vise	[ɔ 'visə]
to tell (vt)	å fortelle	[ɔ fɔ:'tɛlə]

to find (vt)	å finne	[ɔ 'finə]
to get lost (lose one's way)	å gå seg bort	[ɔ 'gɔ sæj 'buːʈ]
map (e.g. underground ~)	kart, linjekart (n)	['kɑːʈ], ['linjə'kɑːʈ]
map (e.g. city ~)	kart (n)	['kɑːʈ]
souvenir, gift	suvenir (m)	[sʉve'nir]
gift shop	suvenirbutikk (m)	[sʉve'nir bʉ'tik]
to take pictures	å fotografere	[ɔ fɔtɔgrɑ'ferə]
to have one's picture taken	å bli fotografert	[ɔ 'bli fɔtɔgrɑ'fɛːʈ]

TRANSPORT

23. Airport

airport	flyplass (m)	['fly,plɑs]
aeroplane	fly (n)	['fly]
airline	flyselskap (n)	['flysəl,skɑp]
air traffic controller	flygeleder (m)	['flygə,ledər]
departure	avgang (m)	['ɑv,gɑŋ]
arrival	ankomst (m)	['ɑn,kɔmst]
to arrive (by plane)	å ankomme	[ɔ 'ɑn,kɔmə]
departure time	avgangstid (m/f)	['ɑvgɑŋs,tid]
arrival time	ankomsttid (m/f)	[ɑn'kɔms,tid]
to be delayed	å bli forsinket	[ɔ 'bli fɔ'ʂinkət]
flight delay	avgangsforsinkelse (m)	['ɑvgɑŋs fɔ'ʂinkəlsə]
information board	informasjonstavle (m/f)	[infɔrmɑ'ʂʊns ,tɑvlə]
information	informasjon (m)	[infɔrmɑ'ʂʊn]
to announce (vt)	å meddele	[ɔ 'mɛd,delə]
flight (e.g. next ~)	fly (n)	['fly]
customs	toll (m)	['tɔl]
customs officer	tollbetjent (m)	['tɔlbe,tjɛnt]
customs declaration	tolldeklarasjon (m)	['tɔldɛklɑrɑ'ʂʊn]
to fill in (vt)	å utfylle	[ɔ 'ʉt,fylə]
to fill in the declaration	å utfylle en tolldeklarasjon	[ɔ 'ʉt,fylə en 'tɔldɛklɑrɑ,ʂʊn]
passport control	passkontroll (m)	['pɑskʊn,trɔl]
luggage	bagasje (m)	[bɑ'gɑʂə]
hand luggage	håndbagasje (m)	['hɔn,bɑ'gɑʂə]
luggage trolley	bagasjetralle (m/f)	[bɑ'gɑʂə,trɑlə]
landing	landing (m)	['lɑniŋ]
landing strip	landingsbane (m)	['lɑniŋs,bɑnə]
to land (vi)	å lande	[ɔ 'lɑnə]
airstairs	trapp (m/f)	['trɑp]
check-in	innsjekking (m/f)	['in,ʂɛkiŋ]
check-in counter	innsjekkingsskranke (m)	['in,ʂɛkiŋs ,skrɑnkə]
to check-in (vi)	å sjekke inn	[ɔ 'ʂɛkə in]
boarding card	boardingkort (n)	['bɔ:diŋ,kɔ:t]
departure gate	gate (m/f)	['gejt]
transit	transitt (m)	[trɑn'sit]
to wait (vt)	å vente	[ɔ 'vɛntə]
departure lounge	ventehall (m)	['vɛntə,hɑl]

| to see off | å ta avskjed | [ɔ 'tɑ 'ɑfˌʂɛd] |
| to say goodbye | å si farvel | [ɔ 'si fɑr'vɛl] |

24. Aeroplane

aeroplane	fly (n)	['fly]
air ticket	flybillett (m)	['fly bi'let]
airline	flyselskap (n)	['flyselˌskɑp]
airport	flyplass (m)	['flyˌplɑs]
supersonic (adj)	overlyds-	['ɔveˌlyds-]

captain	kaptein (m)	[kɑp'tæjn]
crew	besetning (m/f)	[be'sɛtniŋ]
pilot	pilot (m)	[pi'lɔt]
stewardess	flyvertinne (m/f)	[flyvɛ:'ʈinə]
navigator	styrmann (m)	['styrˌmɑn]

wings	vinger (m pl)	['viŋər]
tail	hale (m)	['hɑlə]
cockpit	cockpit, førerkabin (m)	['kɔkpit], ['førərkɑˌbin]
engine	motor (m)	['mɔtʊr]
undercarriage (landing gear)	landingshjul (n)	['lɑniŋsˌjʉl]
turbine	turbin (m)	[tʉr'bin]
propeller	propell (m)	[prʊ'pɛl]
black box	svart boks (m)	['svɑ:ʈ bɔks]
yoke (control column)	ratt (n)	['rɑt]
fuel	brensel (n)	['brɛnsəl]

safety card	sikkerhetsbrosjyre (m)	['sikərhɛtsˌbrɔ'ʂyrə]
oxygen mask	oksygenmaske (m/f)	['ɔksygənˌmɑskə]
uniform	uniform (m)	[ʉni'fɔrm]
lifejacket	redningsvest (m)	['rɛdniŋsˌvɛst]
parachute	fallskjerm (m)	['fɑlˌʂærm]
takeoff	start (m)	['stɑ:ʈ]
to take off (vi)	å løfte	[ɔ 'lœftə]
runway	startbane (m)	['stɑ:ʈˌbɑnə]

visibility	siktbarhet (m)	['siktbɑrˌhet]
flight (act of flying)	flyging (m/f)	['flygiŋ]
altitude	høyde (m)	['højdə]
air pocket	lufthull (n)	['lʉftˌhʉl]

seat	plass (m)	['plɑs]
headphones	hodetelefoner (n pl)	['hodəteləˌfʊnər]
folding tray (tray table)	klappbord (n)	['klɑpˌbʊr]
airplane window	vindu (n)	['vindʉ]
aisle	midtgang (m)	['mitˌgɑŋ]

25. Train

| train | tog (n) | ['tɔg] |
| commuter train | lokaltog (n) | [lɔ'kɑlˌtɔg] |

express train	ekspresstog (n)	[ɛks'prɛsˌtɔg]
diesel locomotive	diesellokomotiv (n)	['disəl lukɔmɔ'tiv]
steam locomotive	damplokomotiv (n)	['damp lukɔmɔ'tiv]

| coach, carriage | vogn (m) | ['vɔŋn] |
| buffet car | restaurantvogn (m/f) | [rɛstʉ'raŋˌvɔŋn] |

rails	skinner (m/f pl)	['ʂinər]
railway	jernbane (m)	['jæːˌn̩banə]
sleeper (track support)	sville (m/f)	['svilə]

platform (railway ~)	perrong, plattform (m/f)	[pɛ'rɔŋ], ['platfɔrm]
platform (~ 1, 2, etc.)	spor (n)	['spʉr]
semaphore	semafor (m)	[sema'fʉr]
station	stasjon (m)	[sta'ʂʉn]

train driver	lokfører (m)	['lukˌførər]
porter (of luggage)	bærer (m)	['bærər]
carriage attendant	betjent (m)	['be'tjɛnt]
passenger	passasjer (m)	[pasa'ʂɛr]
ticket inspector	billett inspektør (m)	[bi'let inspɛk'tør]

corridor (in train)	korridor (m)	[kʉri'dɔr]
emergency brake	nødbrems (m)	['nødˌbrɛms]
compartment	kupé (m)	[kʉ'pe]
berth	køye (m/f)	['køjə]
upper berth	overkøye (m/f)	['ɔvərˌkøjə]
lower berth	underkøye (m/f)	['ʉnərˌkøjə]
bed linen, bedding	sengetøy (n)	['sɛŋəˌtøj]

ticket	billett (m)	[bi'let]
timetable	rutetabell (m)	['rʉtəˌta'bɛl]
information display	informasjonstavle (m/f)	[infɔrma'ʂʉns ˌtavlə]

to leave, to depart	å avgå	[ɔ 'avgɔ]
departure (of train)	avgang (m)	['avˌgaŋ]
to arrive (ab. train)	å ankomme	[ɔ 'anˌkɔmə]
arrival	ankomst (m)	['anˌkɔmst]

to arrive by train	å ankomme med toget	[ɔ 'anˌkɔmə me 'tɔgə]
to get on the train	å gå på toget	[ɔ 'gɔ pɔ 'tɔgə]
to get off the train	å gå av toget	[ɔ 'gɔ ɑ: 'tɔgə]

train crash	togulykke (m/n)	['tɔg ʉ'lʏkə]
to derail (vi)	å spore av	[ɔ 'spʉrə ɑ:]
steam locomotive	damplokomotiv (n)	['damp lukɔmɔ'tiv]
stoker, fireman	fyrbøter (m)	['fyrˌbøtər]
firebox	fyrrom (n)	['fyrˌrʉm]
coal	kull (n)	['kʉl]

26. Ship

| ship | skip (n) | ['ʂip] |
| vessel | fartøy (n) | ['fɑːˌtøj] |

steamship	dampskip (n)	['damp,sip]
riverboat	elvebåt (m)	['ɛlvə,bot]
cruise ship	cruiseskip (n)	['krʉs,sip]
cruiser	krysser (m)	['krʏsər]

yacht	jakt (m/f)	['jakt]
tugboat	bukserbåt (m)	[bʉk'ser,bot]
barge	lastepram (m)	['lastə,pram]
ferry	ferje, ferge (m/f)	['færjə], ['færgə]

| sailing ship | seilbåt (n) | ['sæjl,bot] |
| brigantine | brigantin (m) | [brigan'tin] |

| ice breaker | isbryter (m) | ['is,brytər] |
| submarine | ubåt (m) | ['ʉː,bot] |

boat (flat-bottomed ~)	båt (m)	['bot]
dinghy	jolle (m/f)	['jolə]
lifeboat	livbåt (m)	['liv,bot]
motorboat	motorbåt (m)	['motʉr,bot]

captain	kaptein (m)	[kap'tæjn]
seaman	matros (m)	[ma'trʊs]
sailor	sjømann (m)	['ʂø,man]
crew	besetning (m/f)	[be'sɛtniŋ]

boatswain	båtsmann (m)	['bos,man]
ship's boy	skipsgutt, jungmann (m)	['sips,gʉt], ['jʉŋ,man]
cook	kokk (m)	['kʊk]
ship's doctor	skipslege (m)	['sips,legə]

deck	dekk (n)	['dɛk]
mast	mast (m/f)	['mast]
sail	seil (n)	['sæjl]

hold	lasterom (n)	['lastə,rʊm]
bow (prow)	baug (m)	['bæu]
stern	akterende (m)	['aktə,rɛnə]
oar	åre (m)	['oːrə]
screw propeller	propell (m)	[prʊ'pɛl]

cabin	hytte (m)	['hʏtə]
wardroom	offisersmesse (m/f)	[ofi'sɛrs,mɛsə]
engine room	maskinrom (n)	[ma'ʂin,rʊm]
bridge	kommandobro (m/f)	[kɔ'mandʉ,brʉ]
radio room	radiorom (m)	['radiʉ,rʊm]
wave (radio)	bølge (m)	['bølgə]
logbook	loggbok (m/f)	['log,bʊk]

spyglass	langkikkert (m)	['laŋ,kikeːt]
bell	klokke (m/f)	['klɔkə]
flag	flagg (n)	['flag]

hawser (mooring ~)	trosse (m/f)	['trʊsə]
knot (bowline, etc.)	knute (m)	['knʉtə]
deckrails	rekkverk (n)	['rɛk,værk]

gangway	landgang (m)	['lɑnˌgɑŋ]
anchor	anker (n)	['ɑnkər]
to weigh anchor	å lette anker	[ɔ 'letə 'ɑnkər]
to drop anchor	å kaste anker	[ɔ 'kɑstə 'ɑnkər]
anchor chain	ankerkjetting (m)	['ɑnkərˌçɛtiŋ]

port (harbour)	havn (m/f)	['hɑvn]
quay, wharf	kai (m/f)	['kɑj]
to berth (moor)	å fortøye	[ɔ fɔːˈtøjə]
to cast off	å kaste loss	[ɔ 'kɑstə lɔs]

trip, voyage	reise (m/f)	['ræjsə]
cruise (sea trip)	cruise (n)	['krʉs]
course (route)	kurs (m)	['kʉʂ]
route (itinerary)	rute (m/f)	['rʉtə]

fairway (safe water channel)	seilrende (m)	['sæjlˌrɛnə]
shallows	grunne (m/f)	['grʉnə]
to run aground	å gå på grunn	[ɔ 'gɔ pɔ 'grʉn]

storm	storm (m)	['stɔrm]
signal	signal (n)	[siŋ'nɑl]
to sink (vi)	å synke	[ɔ 'synkə]
Man overboard!	Mann over bord!	['mɑn ˌɔvər 'bʉr]
SOS (distress signal)	SOS (n)	[ɛsʉ'ɛs]
ring buoy	livbøye (m/f)	['livˌbøjə]

CITY

27. Urban transport

bus, coach	buss (m)	['bus]
tram	trikk (m)	['trik]
trolleybus	trolleybuss (m)	['trɔli̩bus]
route (of bus, etc.)	rute (m/f)	['rutə]
number (e.g. bus ~)	nummer (n)	['numər]
to go by ...	å kjøre med ...	[ɔ 'çœːrə me ...]
to get on (~ the bus)	å gå på ...	[ɔ 'gɔ pɔ ...]
to get off ...	å gå av ...	[ɔ 'gɔ ɑː ...]
stop (e.g. bus ~)	holdeplass (m)	['hɔlə̩plɑs]
next stop	neste holdeplass (m)	['nɛstə 'hɔlə̩plɑs]
terminus	endestasjon (m)	['ɛnə̩stɑ'ʂun]
timetable	rutetabell (m)	['rutə̩tɑ'bɛl]
to wait (vt)	å vente	[ɔ 'vɛntə]
ticket	billett (m)	[bi'let]
fare	billettpris (m)	[bi'let̩pris]
cashier (ticket seller)	kasserer (m)	[kɑ'serər]
ticket inspection	billettkontroll (m)	[bi'let kun̩trɔl]
ticket inspector	billett inspektør (m)	[bi'let inspɛk'tør]
to be late (for ...)	å komme for sent	[ɔ 'kɔmə fɔ'ʂɛnt]
to miss (~ the train, etc.)	å komme for sent til ...	[ɔ 'kɔmə fɔ'ʂɛnt til ...]
to be in a hurry	å skynde seg	[ɔ 'ʂynə sæj]
taxi, cab	drosje (m/f), taxi (m)	['drɔʂɛ], ['tɑksi]
taxi driver	taxisjåfør (m)	['tɑksi ʂɔ'før]
by taxi	med taxi	[me 'tɑksi]
taxi rank	taxiholdeplass (m)	['tɑksi 'hɔlə̩plɑs]
to call a taxi	å taxi bestellen	[ɔ 'tɑksi be'stɛlən]
to take a taxi	å ta taxi	[ɔ 'tɑ ̩tɑksi]
traffic	trafikk (m)	[trɑ'fik]
traffic jam	trafikkork (m)	[trɑ'fik̩kɔrk]
rush hour	rushtid (m/f)	['ruʂ̩tid]
to park (vi)	å parkere	[ɔ pɑr'kerə]
to park (vt)	å parkere	[ɔ pɑr'kerə]
car park	parkeringsplass (m)	[pɑr'keriŋs̩plɑs]
underground, tube	tunnelbane, T-bane (m)	['tunəl̩bɑnə], ['tɛː̩bɑnə]
station	stasjon (m)	[stɑ'ʂun]
to take the tube	å kjøre med T-bane	[ɔ 'çœːrə me 'tɛː̩bɑnə]
train	tog (n)	['tɔg]
train station	togstasjon (m)	['tɔg̩stɑ'ʂun]

37

28. City. Life in the city

city, town	by (m)	['by]
capital city	hovedstad (m)	['huvəd,stad]
village	landsby (m)	['lans,by]
city map	bykart (n)	['by,kɑːt]
city centre	sentrum (n)	['sɛntrum]
suburb	forstad (m)	['fɔ,ṣtad]
suburban (adj)	forstads-	['fɔ,ṣtads-]
outskirts	utkant (m)	['ʉt,kant]
environs (suburbs)	omegner (m pl)	['ɔm,æejnər]
city block	kvarter (n)	[kvɑːṭer]
residential block (area)	boligkvarter (n)	['buli,kvɑː'ṭer]
traffic	trafikk (m)	[trɑ'fik]
traffic lights	trafikklys (n)	[trɑ'fik,lys]
public transport	offentlig transport (m)	['ɔfentli trans'pɔːṭ]
crossroads	veikryss (n)	['væjkrʏs]
zebra crossing	fotgjengerovergang (m)	['fʉtjɛŋer 'ɔvər,gɑŋ]
pedestrian subway	undergang (m)	['ʉnər,gɑŋ]
to cross (~ the street)	å gå over	[ɔ 'gɔ 'ɔvər]
pedestrian	fotgjenger (m)	['fʉtjɛŋer]
pavement	fortau (n)	['fɔː,ṭɑʉ]
bridge	bro (m/f)	['brʉ]
embankment (river walk)	kai (m/f)	['kɑj]
fountain	fontene (m)	['funtnə]
allée (garden walkway)	allé (m)	[ɑ'leː]
park	park (m)	['pɑrk]
boulevard	bulevard (m)	[bule'vɑr]
square	torg (n)	['tɔr]
avenue (wide street)	aveny (m)	[ɑve'ny]
street	gate (m/f)	['gɑtə]
side street	sidegate (m/f)	['sidə,gɑtə]
dead end	blindgate (m/f)	['blin,gɑtə]
house	hus (n)	['hʉs]
building	bygning (m/f)	['bygniŋ]
skyscraper	skyskraper (m)	['ṣy,skrɑpər]
facade	fasade (m)	[fɑ'sɑdə]
roof	tak (n)	['tɑk]
window	vindu (n)	['vindʉ]
arch	bue (m)	['bʉːə]
column	søyle (m)	['søjlə]
corner	hjørne (n)	['jœːɳə]
shop window	utstillingsvindu (n)	['ʉt,stiliŋs 'vindʉ]
signboard (store sign, etc.)	skilt (n)	['ṣilt]
poster	plakat (m)	[plɑ'kat]
advertising poster	reklameplakat (m)	[rɛ'klɑmə,plɑ'kat]

hoarding	reklametavle (m/f)	[rɛ'klaməˌtɑvlə]
rubbish	søppel (m/f/n), avfall (n)	['sœpəl], ['ɑvˌfɑl]
rubbish bin	søppelkasse (m/f)	['sœpəlˌkɑsə]
to litter (vi)	å kaste søppel	[ɔ 'kɑstə 'sœpəl]
rubbish dump	søppelfylling (m/f), deponi (n)	['sœpəlˌfʏliŋ], [ˌdepɔ'ni]

telephone box	telefonboks (m)	[tele'funˌbɔks]
lamppost	lyktestolpe (m)	['lʏktəˌstɔlpə]
bench (park ~)	benk (m)	['bɛŋk]

police officer	politi (m)	[pʊli'ti]
police	politi (n)	[pʊli'ti]
beggar	tigger (m)	['tigər]
homeless (n)	hjemløs	['jɛmˌløs]

29. Urban institutions

shop	forretning, butikk (m)	[fɔ'rɛtniŋ], [bʉ'tik]
chemist, pharmacy	apotek (n)	[apʊ'tek]
optician (spectacles shop)	optikk (m)	[ɔp'tik]
shopping centre	kjøpesenter (n)	['çœpəˌsɛntər]
supermarket	supermarked (n)	['sʉpəˌmɑrket]

bakery	bakeri (n)	[bɑke'ri]
baker	baker (m)	['bɑkər]
cake shop	konditori (n)	[kʊnditɔ'ri]
grocery shop	matbutikk (m)	['mɑtbʉˌtik]
butcher shop	slakterbutikk (m)	['ʂlɑktəbʉˌtik]

greengrocer	grønnsaksbutikk (m)	['grœnˌsɑks bʉ'tik]
market	marked (n)	['mɑrkəd]

coffee bar	kafé, kaffebar (m)	[kɑ'fe], ['kɑfəˌbɑr]
restaurant	restaurant (m)	[rɛstʉ'rɑŋ]
pub, bar	pub (m)	['pʉb]
pizzeria	pizzeria (m)	[pitse'riɑ]

hairdresser	frisørsalong (m)	[fri'sør sɑˌlɔŋ]
post office	post (m)	['pɔst]
dry cleaners	renseri (n)	[rɛnse'ri]
photo studio	fotostudio (n)	['fotoˌstʉdiɔ]

shoe shop	skobutikk (m)	['skʊˌbʉ'tik]
bookshop	bokhandel (m)	['bʊkˌhɑndəl]
sports shop	idrettsbutikk (m)	['idrɛts bʉ'tik]

clothes repair shop	reparasjon (m) av klær	[repɑrɑ'ʂʊn ɑ: ˌklær]
formal wear hire	leie (m/f) av klær	['læjə ɑ: ˌklær]
video rental shop	filmutleie (m/f)	['filmˌʉt'læjə]

circus	sirkus (m/n)	['sirkʉs]
zoo	zoo, dyrepark (m)	['sʊ:], [dyrə'pɑrk]
cinema	kino (m)	['çinʊ]
museum	museum (n)	[mʉ'seum]

library	bibliotek (n)	[biblio'tek]
theatre	teater (n)	[te'atər]
opera (opera house)	opera (m)	['opera]
nightclub	nattklubb (m)	['nat,klʉb]
casino	kasino (n)	[ka'sinʉ]

mosque	moské (m)	[mʉ'ske]
synagogue	synagoge (m)	[syna'gʉgə]
cathedral	katedral (m)	[kate'dral]
temple	tempel (n)	['tɛmpəl]
church	kirke (m/f)	['çirkə]

college	institutt (n)	[insti'tʉt]
university	universitet (n)	[ʉnivæʂi'tet]
school	skole (m/f)	['skʉlə]

prefecture	prefektur (n)	[prɛfɛk'tʉr]
town hall	rådhus (n)	['rɔd,hʉs]
hotel	hotell (n)	[hʉ'tɛl]
bank	bank (m)	['bank]

embassy	ambassade (m)	[amba'sadə]
travel agency	reisebyrå (n)	['ræjsə by,rɔ]
information office	opplysningskontor (n)	[ɔp'lʏsniŋs kʉn'tʉr]
currency exchange	vekslingskontor (n)	['vɛkʂliŋs kʉn'tʉr]

| underground, tube | tunnelbane, T-bane (m) | ['tʉnəl,banə], ['tɛː,banə] |
| hospital | sykehus (n) | ['sykə,hʉs] |

| petrol station | bensinstasjon (m) | [bɛn'sin,sta'ʂʉn] |
| car park | parkeringsplass (m) | [par'keriŋs,plas] |

30. Signs

signboard (store sign, etc.)	skilt (n)	['ʂilt]
notice (door sign, etc.)	innskrift (m/f)	['in,skrift]
poster	plakat, poster (m)	['pla,kat], ['postər]
direction sign	veiviser (m)	['væj,visər]
arrow (sign)	pil (m/f)	['pil]

caution	advarsel (m)	['ad,vaʂəl]
warning sign	varselskilt (n)	['vaʂəl,ʂilt]
to warn (vt)	å varsle	[ɔ 'vaʂlə]

rest day (weekly ~)	fridag (m)	['fri,da]
timetable (schedule)	rutetabell (m)	['rʉtə,ta'bɛl]
opening hours	åpningstider (m/f pl)	['ɔpniŋs,tidər]

WELCOME!	VELKOMMEN!	['vɛl,kɔmən]
ENTRANCE	INNGANG	['in,gaŋ]
WAY OUT	UTGANG	['ʉt,gaŋ]

| PUSH | SKYV | ['ʂyv] |
| PULL | TREKK | ['trɛk] |

| OPEN | ÅPENT | ['ɔpənt] |
| CLOSED | STENGT | ['stɛŋt] |

| WOMEN | DAMER | ['damər] |
| MEN | HERRER | ['hærər] |

DISCOUNTS	RABATT	[ra'bat]
SALE	SALG	['salg]
NEW!	NYTT!	['nʏt]
FREE	GRATIS	['gratis]

ATTENTION!	FORSIKTIG!	[fʊ'ʂiktə]
NO VACANCIES	INGEN LEDIGE ROM	['iŋən 'lediə rʊm]
RESERVED	RESERVERT	[resɛr'vɛːt]

| ADMINISTRATION | ADMINISTRASJON | [administrɑ'ʂʊn] |
| STAFF ONLY | KUN FOR ANSATTE | ['kʉn fɔr an'satə] |

BEWARE OF THE DOG!	VOKT DEM FOR HUNDEN	['vɔkt dem fɔ 'hʉnən]
NO SMOKING	RØYKING FORBUDT	['røjkiŋ fɔr'bʉt]
DO NOT TOUCH!	IKKE RØR!	['ikə 'rør]

DANGEROUS	FARLIG	['faːli]
DANGER	FARE	['farə]
HIGH VOLTAGE	HØYSPENNING	['høj,spɛniŋ]
NO SWIMMING!	BADING FORBUDT	['badiŋ fɔr'bʉt]
OUT OF ORDER	I USTAND	[i 'ʉ,stan]

FLAMMABLE	BRANNFARLIG	['bran,faːli]
FORBIDDEN	FORBUDT	[fɔr'bʉt]
NO TRESPASSING!	INGEN INNKJØRING	['iŋən 'in,çœriŋ]
WET PAINT	NYMALT	['ny,malt]

31. Shopping

to buy (purchase)	å kjøpe	[ɔ 'çœːpə]
shopping	innkjøp (n)	['in,çœp]
to go shopping	å gå shopping	[ɔ gɔ ,sopiŋ]
shopping	shopping (m)	['ʂopiŋ]

| to be open (ab. shop) | å være åpen | [ɔ 'værə 'ɔpən] |
| to be closed | å være stengt | [ɔ 'værə 'stɛŋt] |

footwear, shoes	skotøy (n)	['skʊtøj]
clothes, clothing	klær (n)	['klær]
cosmetics	kosmetikk (m)	[kʊsme'tik]
food products	matvarer (m/f pl)	['mat,varər]
gift, present	gave (m/f)	['gɑvə]

| shop assistant (masc.) | forselger (m) | [fɔ'ʂɛlər] |
| shop assistant (fem.) | forselger (m) | [fɔ'ʂɛlər] |

| cash desk | kasse (m/f) | ['kasə] |
| mirror | speil (n) | ['spæjl] |

41

| counter (shop ~) | disk (m) | ['disk] |
| fitting room | prøverom (n) | ['prøvəˌrʊm] |

to try on	å prøve	[ɔ 'prøvə]
to fit (ab. dress, etc.)	å passe	[ɔ 'pɑsə]
to fancy (vt)	å like	[ɔ 'likə]

price	pris (m)	['pris]
price tag	prislapp (m)	['prisˌlɑp]
to cost (vt)	å koste	[ɔ 'kɔstə]
How much?	Hvor mye?	[vʊr 'mye]
discount	rabatt (m)	[rɑ'bɑt]

inexpensive (adj)	billig	['bili]
cheap (adj)	billig	['bili]
expensive (adj)	dyr	['dyr]
It's expensive	Det er dyrt	[de ær 'dy:t]

hire (n)	utleie (m/f)	['ʉtˌlæje]
to hire (~ a dinner jacket)	å leie	[ɔ 'læjə]
credit (trade credit)	kreditt (m)	[krɛ'dit]
on credit (adv)	på kreditt	[pɔ krɛ'dit]

CLOTHING & ACCESSORIES

32. Outerwear. Coats

clothes	klær (n)	['klær]
outerwear	yttertøy (n)	['ytə,tøj]
winter clothing	vinterklær (n pl)	['vinter,klær]
coat (overcoat)	frakk (m), kåpe (m/f)	['frɑk], ['ko:pə]
fur coat	pels (m), pelskåpe (m/f)	['pɛls], ['pɛls,ko:pə]
fur jacket	pelsjakke (m/f)	['pɛls,jakə]
down coat	dunjakke (m/f)	['dʉn,jakə]
jacket (e.g. leather ~)	jakke (m/f)	['jakə]
raincoat (trenchcoat, etc.)	regnfrakk (m)	['ræjn,frɑk]
waterproof (adj)	vanntett	['vɑn,tɛt]

33. Men's & women's clothing

shirt (button shirt)	skjorte (m/f)	['sœ:tə]
trousers	bukse (m)	['bʉksə]
jeans	jeans (m)	['dʒins]
suit jacket	dressjakke (m/f)	['drɛs,jakə]
suit	dress (m)	['drɛs]
dress (frock)	kjole (m)	['çulə]
skirt	skjørt (n)	['sø:t]
blouse	bluse (m)	['blʉsə]
knitted jacket (cardigan, etc.)	strikket trøye (m/f)	['strikə 'trøjə]
jacket (of woman's suit)	blazer (m)	['blæsər]
T-shirt	T-skjorte (m/f)	['te,sœ:tə]
shorts (short trousers)	shorts (m)	['sɔ:ts]
tracksuit	treningsdrakt (m/f)	['treniŋs,drɑkt]
bathrobe	badekåpe (m/f)	['bɑdə,ko:pə]
pyjamas	pyjamas (m)	[py'sɑmɑs]
jumper (sweater)	sweater (m)	['svɛtər]
pullover	pullover (m)	[pʉ'lɔvər]
waistcoat	vest (m)	['vɛst]
tailcoat	livkjole (m)	['liv,çulə]
dinner suit	smoking (m)	['smɔkiŋ]
uniform	uniform (m)	[ʉni'fɔrm]
workwear	arbeidsklær (n pl)	['ɑrbæjds,klær]
boiler suit	kjeledress, overall (m)	['çelə,drɛs], ['ɔvɛr,ɔl]
coat (e.g. doctor's smock)	kittel (m)	['çitəl]

34. Clothing. Underwear

underwear	undertøy (n)	['ʉnəˌtøj]
pants	underbukse (m/f)	['ʉnərˌbʉksə]
panties	truse (m/f)	['trʉsə]
vest (singlet)	undertrøye (m/f)	['ʉnəˌtrøjə]
socks	sokker (m pl)	['sɔkər]
nightgown	nattkjole (m)	['natˌçulə]
bra	behå (m)	['bəˌhɔ]
knee highs (knee-high socks)	knestrømper (m/f pl)	['knɛˌstrømpər]
tights	strømpebukse (m/f)	['strømpəˌbʉksə]
stockings (hold ups)	strømper (m/f pl)	['strømpər]
swimsuit, bikini	badedrakt (m/f)	['badəˌdrakt]

35. Headwear

hat	hatt (m)	['hat]
trilby hat	hatt (m)	['hat]
baseball cap	baseball cap (m)	['bɛjsbɔl kɛp]
flatcap	sikspens (m)	['sikspens]
beret	alpelue, baskerlue (m/f)	['alpəˌlʉə], ['baskəˌlʉə]
hood	hette (m/f)	['hɛtə]
panama hat	panamahatt (m)	['panamaˌhat]
knit cap (knitted hat)	strikket lue (m/f)	['strikəˌlʉə]
headscarf	skaut (n)	['skaʊt]
women's hat	hatt (m)	['hat]
hard hat	hjelm (m)	['jɛlm]
forage cap	båtlue (m/f)	['bɔtˌlʉə]
helmet	hjelm (m)	['jɛlm]
bowler	bowlerhatt, skalk (m)	['boʊlerˌhat], ['skalk]
top hat	flosshatt (m)	['flɔsˌhat]

36. Footwear

footwear	skotøy (n)	['skʊtøj]
shoes (men's shoes)	skor (m pl)	['skʊr]
shoes (women's shoes)	pumps (m pl)	['pʉmps]
boots (e.g., cowboy ~)	støvler (m pl)	['støvlər]
carpet slippers	tøfler (m pl)	['tøflər]
trainers	tennissko (m pl)	['tɛnisˌskʊ]
trainers	canvas sko (m pl)	['kanvas ˌskʊ]
sandals	sandaler (m pl)	[san'dalər]
cobbler (shoe repairer)	skomaker (m)	['skʊˌmakər]
heel	hæl (m)	['hæl]

pair (of shoes)	par (n)	['pɑr]
lace (shoelace)	skolisse (m/f)	['skʊˌlisə]
to lace up (vt)	å snøre	[ɔ 'snørə]
shoehorn	skohorn (n)	['skʊˌhuːn]
shoe polish	skokrem (m)	['skʊˌkrɛm]

37. Personal accessories

gloves	hansker (m pl)	['hanskər]
mittens	votter (m pl)	['vɔtər]
scarf (muffler)	skjerf (n)	['ʂærf]

glasses	briller (m pl)	['brilər]
frame (eyeglass ~)	innfatning (m/f)	['inˌfatniŋ]
umbrella	paraply (m)	[parɑ'ply]
walking stick	stokk (m)	['stɔk]
hairbrush	hårbørste (m)	['hɔrˌbœʂtə]
fan	vifte (m/f)	['viftə]

tie (necktie)	slips (n)	['slips]
bow tie	sløyfe (m/f)	['ʂløjfə]
braces	bukseseler (m pl)	['bʉksə'selər]
handkerchief	lommetørkle (n)	['lʊməˌtœrklə]

comb	kam (m)	['kam]
hair slide	hårspenne (m/f/n)	['hoːrˌspɛnə]
hairpin	hårnål (m/f)	['hoːrˌnɔl]
buckle	spenne (m/f/n)	['spɛnə]

| belt | belte (m) | ['bɛltə] |
| shoulder strap | skulderreim, rem (m/f) | ['skʉldəˌræjm], ['rem] |

bag (handbag)	veske (m/f)	['vɛskə]
handbag	håndveske (m/f)	['hɔnˌvɛskə]
rucksack	ryggsekk (m)	['rʏgˌsɛk]

38. Clothing. Miscellaneous

fashion	mote (m)	['mʊtə]
in vogue (adj)	moteriktig	['mʊtəˌrikti]
fashion designer	moteskaper (m)	['mʊtəˌskɑpər]

collar	krage (m)	['krɑgə]
pocket	lomme (m/f)	['lʊmə]
pocket (as adj)	lomme-	['lʊmə-]
sleeve	erme (n)	['ærmə]
hanging loop	hempe (m)	['hɛmpə]
flies (on trousers)	gylf, buksesmekk (m)	['gylf], ['bʉksəˌsmɛk]

zip (fastener)	glidelås (m/n)	['glidəˌlɔs]
fastener	hekte (m/f), knepping (m)	['hɛktə], ['knɛpiŋ]
button	knapp (m)	['knɑp]

| buttonhole | klapphull (n) | ['klap,hʉl] |
| to come off (ab. button) | å falle av | [ɔ 'falə a:] |

to sew (vi, vt)	å sy	[ɔ 'sy]
to embroider (vi, vt)	å brodere	[ɔ brʉ'derə]
embroidery	broderi (n)	[brʉde'ri]
sewing needle	synål (m/f)	['sy,nɔl]
thread	tråd (m)	['trɔ]
seam	søm (m)	['søm]

to get dirty (vi)	å skitne seg til	[ɔ 'şitnə sæj til]
stain (mark, spot)	flekk (m)	['flek]
to crease, crumple (vi)	å bli skrukkete	[ɔ 'bli 'skrʉketə]
to tear, to rip (vt)	å rive	[ɔ 'rivə]
clothes moth	møll (m/n)	['møl]

39. Personal care. Cosmetics

toothpaste	tannpasta (m)	['tan,pasta]
toothbrush	tannbørste (m)	['tan,bœştə]
to clean one's teeth	å pusse tennene	[ɔ 'pʉsə 'tɛnənə]

razor	høvel (m)	['høvəl]
shaving cream	barberkrem (m)	[bar'bɛr,krɛm]
to shave (vi)	å barbere seg	[ɔ bar'berə sæj]

| soap | såpe (m/f) | ['so:pə] |
| shampoo | sjampo (m) | ['şam,pʉ] |

scissors	saks (m/f)	['saks]
nail file	neglefil (m/f)	['nɛjlə,fil]
nail clippers	negleklipper (m)	['nɛjlə,klipər]
tweezers	pinsett (m)	[pin'sɛt]

cosmetics	kosmetikk (m)	[kʉsme'tik]
face mask	ansiktsmaske (m/f)	['ansikts,maskə]
manicure	manikyr (m)	[mani'kyr]
to have a manicure	å få manikyr	[ɔ 'fɔ mani'kyr]
pedicure	pedikyr (m)	[pedi'kyr]

make-up bag	sminkeveske (m/f)	['sminkə,vɛskə]
face powder	pudder (n)	['pʉdər]
powder compact	pudderdåse (m)	['pʉdər,do:sə]
blusher	rouge (m)	['ru:ş]

perfume (bottled)	parfyme (m)	[par'fymə]
toilet water (lotion)	eau de toilette (m)	['ɔ: də twa'let]
lotion	lotion (m)	['loʉşɛn]
cologne	eau de cologne (m)	['ɔ: də kɔ'lɔɲ]

eyeshadow	øyeskygge (m)	['øjə,sygə]
eyeliner	eyeliner (m)	['a:j,lajnər]
mascara	maskara (m)	[ma'skara]
lipstick	leppestift (m)	['lepə,stift]

nail polish	neglelakk (m)	['nɛjlə‚lɑk]
hair spray	hårlakk (m)	['hoːr‚lɑk]
deodorant	deodorant (m)	[deudʋ'rɑnt]

cream	krem (m)	['krɛm]
face cream	ansiktskrem (m)	['ɑnsikts‚krɛm]
hand cream	håndkrem (m)	['hɔn‚krɛm]
anti-wrinkle cream	antirynkekrem (m)	[ɑnti'rʏnkə‚krɛm]
day cream	dagkrem (m)	['dɑg‚krɛm]
night cream	nattkrem (m)	['nɑt‚krɛm]
day (as adj)	dag-	['dɑg-]
night (as adj)	natt-	['nɑt-]

tampon	tampong (m)	[tɑm'pɔŋ]
toilet paper (toilet roll)	toalettpapir (n)	[tʋɑ'let pɑ'pir]
hair dryer	hårføner (m)	['hoːr‚fønər]

40. Watches. Clocks

watch (wristwatch)	armbåndsur (n)	['ɑrmbɔns‚ʉr]
dial	urskive (m/f)	['ʉː‚ʂivə]
hand (of clock, watch)	viser (m)	['visər]
metal bracelet	armbånd (n)	['ɑrm‚bɔn]
watch strap	rem (m/f)	['rem]

battery	batteri (n)	[bɑtɛ'ri]
to be flat (battery)	å bli utladet	[ɔ 'bli 'ʉt‚lɑdət]
to change a battery	å skifte batteriene	[ɔ 'ʂifte bɑtɛ'riene]
to run fast	å gå for fort	[ɔ 'gɔ fɔ 'foːt]
to run slow	å gå for sakte	[ɔ 'gɔ fɔ 'sɑktə]

wall clock	veggur (n)	['vɛg‚ʉr]
hourglass	timeglass (n)	['timə‚glɑs]
sundial	solur (n)	['sʋl‚ʉr]
alarm clock	vekkerklokka (m/f)	['vɛkər‚klɔkɑ]
watchmaker	urmaker (m)	['ʉr‚mɑkər]
to repair (vt)	å reparere	[ɔ repɑ'rerə]

EVERYDAY EXPERIENCE

41. Money

money	penger (m pl)	['pɛŋər]
currency exchange	veksling (m/f)	['vɛkṣliŋ]
exchange rate	kurs (m)	['kuṣ]
cashpoint	minibank (m)	['miniˌbɑnk]
coin	mynt (m)	['mʏnt]
dollar	dollar (m)	['dɔlɑr]
euro	euro (m)	['ɛʉrʉ]
lira	lira (m)	['lire]
Deutschmark	mark (m/f)	['mɑrk]
franc	franc (m)	['frɑn]
pound sterling	pund sterling (m)	['pʉn stɛ:'liŋ]
yen	yen (m)	['jɛn]
debt	skyld (m/f), gjeld (m)	['ṣyl], ['jɛl]
debtor	skyldner (m)	['ṣylnər]
to lend (money)	å låne ut	[ɔ 'lo:nə ʉt]
to borrow (vi, vt)	å låne	[ɔ 'lo:nə]
bank	bank (m)	['bɑnk]
account	konto (m)	['kɔntʉ]
to deposit (vt)	å sette inn	[ɔ 'sɛtə in]
to deposit into the account	å sette inn på kontoen	[ɔ 'sɛtə in pɔ 'kɔntʉən]
to withdraw (vt)	å ta ut fra kontoen	[ɔ 'tɑ ʉt frɑ 'kɔntʉən]
credit card	kredittkort (n)	[krɛ'ditˌkɔ:t]
cash	kontanter (m pl)	[kʉn'tɑntər]
cheque	sjekk (m)	['ṣɛk]
to write a cheque	å skrive en sjekk	[ɔ 'skrivə en 'ṣɛk]
chequebook	sjekkbok (m/f)	['ṣɛkˌbʉk]
wallet	lommebok (m)	['lʉməˌbʉk]
purse	pung (m)	['pʉŋ]
safe	safe, seif (m)	['sɛjf]
heir	arving (m)	['ɑrviŋ]
inheritance	arv (m)	['ɑrv]
fortune (wealth)	formue (m)	['fɔrˌmʉə]
lease	leie (m)	['læje]
rent (money)	husleie (m/f)	['hʉsˌlæje]
to rent (sth from sb)	å leie	[ɔ 'læje]
price	pris (m)	['pris]
cost	kostnad (m)	['kɔstnɑd]

sum	sum (m)	['sʉm]
to spend (vt)	å bruke	[ɔ 'brʉkə]
expenses	utgifter (m/f pl)	['ʉtˌjiftər]
to economize (vi, vt)	å spare	[ɔ 'spɑrə]
economical	sparsom	['spɑʂɔm]
to pay (vi, vt)	å betale	[ɔ be'tɑlə]
payment	betaling (m/f)	[be'tɑliŋ]
change (give the ~)	vekslepenger (pl)	['vɛkʂləˌpɛŋər]
tax	skatt (m)	['skɑt]
fine	bot (m/f)	['bʉt]
to fine (vt)	å bøtelegge	[ɔ 'bøtəˌlegə]

42. Post. Postal service

post office	post (m)	['pɔst]
post (letters, etc.)	post (m)	['pɔst]
postman	postbud (n)	['pɔstˌbʉd]
opening hours	åpningstider (m/f pl)	['ɔpniŋsˌtidər]
letter	brev (n)	['brev]
registered letter	rekommandert brev (n)	[rekʉmɑn'dɛːt ˌbrev]
postcard	postkort (n)	['pɔstˌkɔːt]
telegram	telegram (n)	[tele'grɑm]
parcel	postpakke (m/f)	['pɔstˌpɑkə]
money transfer	pengeoverføring (m/f)	['pɛŋə ˈɔvərˌføriŋ]
to receive (vt)	å motta	[ɔ 'mɔtɑ]
to send (vt)	å sende	[ɔ 'sɛnə]
sending	avsending (m)	['ɑfˌsɛniŋ]
address	adresse (m)	[ɑ'drɛsə]
postcode	postnummer (n)	['pɔstˌnʉmər]
sender	avsender (m)	['ɑfˌsɛnər]
receiver	mottaker (m)	['mɔtˌtɑkər]
name (first name)	fornavn (n)	['fɔrˌnɑvn]
surname (last name)	etternavn (n)	['ɛtəˌnɑvn]
postage rate	tariff (m)	[tɑ'rif]
standard (adj)	vanlig	['vɑnli]
economical (adj)	økonomisk	[økʉ'nɔmisk]
weight	vekt (m)	['vɛkt]
to weigh (~ letters)	å veie	[ɔ 'væjə]
envelope	konvolutt (m)	[kʉnvʉ'lʉt]
postage stamp	frimerke (n)	['friˌmærkə]
to stamp an envelope	å sette på frimerke	[ɔ 'sɛtə pɔ 'friˌmærkə]

43. Banking

| bank | bank (m) | ['bɑnk] |
| branch (of bank, etc.) | avdeling (m) | ['ɑvˌdeliŋ] |

consultant	konsulent (m)	[kʊnsʉ'lent]
manager (director)	forstander (m)	[fo'ʂtandər]
bank account	bankkonto (m)	['bɑŋk͵kɔntʊ]
account number	kontonummer (n)	['kɔntʊ͵nʉmər]
current account	sjekkonto (m)	['ʂɛk͵kɔntʊ]
deposit account	sparekonto (m)	['spɑrə͵kɔntʊ]
to open an account	å åpne en konto	[ɔ 'ɔpnə en 'kɔntʊ]
to close the account	å lukke kontoen	[ɔ 'lʉkə 'kɔntʊən]
to deposit into the account	å sette inn på kontoen	[ɔ 'sɛtə in pɔ 'kɔntʊən]
to withdraw (vt)	å ta ut fra kontoen	[ɔ 'ta ʉt fra 'kɔntʊən]
deposit	innskudd (n)	['in͵skʉd]
to make a deposit	å sette inn	[ɔ 'sɛtə in]
wire transfer	overføring (m/f)	['ɔvər͵føriŋ]
to wire, to transfer	å overføre	[ɔ 'ɔvər͵førə]
sum	sum (m)	['sʉm]
How much?	Hvor mye?	[vʊr 'myə]
signature	underskrift (m/f)	['ʉnə͵skrift]
to sign (vt)	å underskrive	[ɔ 'ʉnə͵skrivə]
credit card	kredittkort (n)	[krɛ'dit͵kɔːʈ]
code (PIN code)	kode (m)	['kʊdə]
credit card number	kreditkortnummer (n)	[krɛ'dit͵kɔːʈ 'nʉmər]
cashpoint	minibank (m)	['mini͵bɑŋk]
cheque	sjekk (m)	['ʂɛk]
to write a cheque	å skrive en sjekk	[ɔ 'skrivə en 'ʂɛk]
chequebook	sjekkbok (m/f)	['ʂɛk͵bʊk]
loan (bank ~)	lån (n)	['lɔn]
to apply for a loan	å søke om lån	[ɔ ͵søkə ɔm 'lɔn]
to get a loan	å få lån	[ɔ 'fɔ 'lɔn]
to give a loan	å gi lån	[ɔ 'ji 'lɔn]
guarantee	garanti (m)	[gɑrɑn'ti]

44. Telephone. Phone conversation

telephone	telefon (m)	[tele'fʊn]
mobile phone	mobiltelefon (m)	[mʊ'bil tele'fʊn]
answerphone	telefonsvarer (m)	[tele'fʊn͵svarər]
to call (by phone)	å ringe	[ɔ 'riŋə]
call, ring	telefonsamtale (m)	[tele'fʊn 'sɑm͵talə]
to dial a number	å slå et nummer	[ɔ 'ʂlɔ et 'nʉmər]
Hello!	Hallo!	[ha'lʊ]
to ask (vt)	å spørre	[ɔ 'spørə]
to answer (vi, vt)	å svare	[ɔ 'svarə]
to hear (vt)	å høre	[ɔ 'hørə]
well (adv)	godt	['gɔt]

| not well (adv) | dårlig | ['doːli] |
| noises (interference) | støy (m) | ['støj] |

receiver	telefonrør (n)	[tele'fʊnˌrør]
to pick up (~ the phone)	å ta telefonen	[ɔ 'ta tele'fʊnən]
to hang up (~ the phone)	å legge på røret	[ɔ 'legə pɔ 'rørə]

busy (engaged)	opptatt	['ɔpˌtat]
to ring (ab. phone)	å ringe	[ɔ 'riŋə]
telephone book	telefonkatalog (m)	[tele'fʊn kata'lɔg]

local (adj)	lokal-	[lɔ'kal-]
local call	lokalsamtale (m)	[lɔ'kal 'samˌtalə]
trunk (e.g. ~ call)	riks-	['riks-]
trunk call	rikssamtale (m)	['riks 'samˌtalə]
international (adj)	internasjonal	['intɛːŋaʂʊˌnal]
international call	internasjonal samtale (m)	['intɛːŋaʂʊˌnal 'samˌtalə]

45. Mobile telephone

mobile phone	mobiltelefon (m)	[mʊ'bil tele'fʊn]
display	skjerm (m)	['ʂærm]
button	knapp (m)	['knap]
SIM card	SIM-kort (n)	['simˌkɔːt]

battery	batteri (n)	[batɛ'ri]
to be flat (battery)	å bli utladet	[ɔ 'bli 'ʉtˌladət]
charger	lader (m)	['ladər]

menu	meny (m)	[me'ny]
settings	innstillinger (m/f pl)	['inˌstiliŋər]
tune (melody)	melodi (m)	[melɔ'di]
to select (vt)	å velge	[ɔ 'vɛlgə]

calculator	regnemaskin (m)	['rɛjnə maˌʂin]
voice mail	telefonsvarer (m)	[tele'fʊnˌsvarər]
alarm clock	vekkerklokka (m/f)	['vɛkərˌklɔka]
contacts	kontakter (m pl)	[kʊn'taktər]

| SMS (text message) | SMS-beskjed (m) | [ɛsɛm'ɛs bɛˌʂɛ] |
| subscriber | abonnent (m) | [abɔ'nɛnt] |

46. Stationery

| ballpoint pen | kulepenn (m) | ['kʉːləˌpɛn] |
| fountain pen | fyllepenn (m) | ['fʏləˌpɛn] |

pencil	blyant (m)	['blyˌant]
highlighter	merkepenn (m)	['mærkəˌpɛn]
felt-tip pen	tusjpenn (m)	['tʉʂˌpɛn]
notepad	notatbok (m/f)	[nʊ'tatˌbʊk]
diary	dagbok (m/f)	['dagˌbʊk]

ruler	linjal (m)	[li'njal]
calculator	regnemaskin (m)	['rɛjnə maˌʂin]
rubber	viskelær (n)	['viskəˌlær]
drawing pin	tegnestift (m)	['tæjnəˌstift]
paper clip	binders (m)	['bindɛʂ]

glue	lim (n)	['lim]
stapler	stiftemaskin (m)	['stiftə maˌʂin]
hole punch	hullemaskin (m)	['hʉlə maˌʂin]
pencil sharpener	blyantspisser (m)	['blyantˌspisər]

47. Foreign languages

language	språk (n)	['sprɔk]
foreign (adj)	fremmed-	['fremə-]
foreign language	fremmedspråk (n)	['fremedˌsprɔk]
to study (vt)	å studere	[ɔ stʉ'derə]
to learn (language, etc.)	å lære	[ɔ 'lærə]

to read (vi, vt)	å lese	[ɔ 'lesə]
to speak (vi, vt)	å tale	[ɔ 'talə]
to understand (vt)	å forstå	[ɔ fɔ'ʂtɔ]
to write (vt)	å skrive	[ɔ 'skrivə]

fast (adv)	fort	['fʊːt]
slowly (adv)	langsomt	['laŋsɔmt]
fluently (adv)	flytende	['flytnə]

rules	regler (m pl)	['rɛglər]
grammar	grammatikk (m)	[grama'tik]
vocabulary	ordforråd (n)	['uːrfʊˌrɔd]
phonetics	fonetikk (m)	[fʊne'tik]

textbook	lærebok (m/f)	['lærəˌbʊk]
dictionary	ordbok (m/f)	['uːrˌbʊk]
teach-yourself book	lærebok (m/f) for selvstudium	['lærəˌbʊk fɔ 'selˌstʉdium]

| phrasebook | parlør (m) | [pɑ:'lør] |

cassette, tape	kassett (m)	[ka'sɛt]
videotape	videokassett (m)	['videʊ ka'sɛt]
CD, compact disc	CD-rom (m)	['sɛdɛˌrʉm]
DVD	DVD (m)	[deve'de]

alphabet	alfabet (n)	[alfa'bet]
to spell (vt)	å stave	[ɔ 'stavə]
pronunciation	uttale (m)	['ʉtˌtalə]

accent	aksent (m)	[ak'saŋ]
with an accent	med aksent	[me ak'saŋ]
without an accent	uten aksent	['ʉtən ak'saŋ]

| word | ord (n) | ['uːr] |
| meaning | betydning (m) | [be'tʏdniŋ] |

course (e.g. a French ~)	**kurs** (n)	['kʉʂ]
to sign up	**å anmelde seg**	[ɔ 'ɑnˌmɛlə sæj]
teacher	**lærer** (m)	['lærər]
translation (process)	**oversettelse** (m)	['ɔveˌsɛtəlsə]
translation (text, etc.)	**oversettelse** (m)	['ɔveˌsɛtəlsə]
translator	**oversetter** (m)	['ɔveˌsɛtər]
interpreter	**tolk** (m)	['tɔlk]
polyglot	**polyglott** (m)	[pʊlʏ'glɔt]
memory	**minne** (n), **hukommelse** (m)	['minə], [hʉ'kɔməlsə]

MEALS. RESTAURANT

48. Table setting

spoon	skje (m)	['ʂe]
knife	kniv (m)	['kniv]
fork	gaffel (m)	['gɑfəl]
cup (e.g., coffee ~)	kopp (m)	['kɔp]
plate (dinner ~)	tallerken (m)	[tɑ'lærkən]
saucer	tefat (n)	['te͵fɑt]
serviette	serviett (m)	[sɛrvi'ɛt]
toothpick	tannpirker (m)	['tɑn͵pirkər]

49. Restaurant

restaurant	restaurant (m)	[rɛstʊ'rɑŋ]
coffee bar	kafé, kaffebar (m)	[kɑ'fe], ['kɑfə͵bɑr]
pub, bar	bar (m)	['bɑr]
tearoom	tesalong (m)	['tesɑ͵lɔŋ]
waiter	servitør (m)	['særvi'tør]
waitress	servitrise (m/f)	[særvi'trisə]
barman	bartender (m)	['bɑː͵tɛndər]
menu	meny (m)	[me'ny]
wine list	vinkart (n)	['vin͵kɑːt]
to book a table	å reservere bord	[ɔ resɛr'verə 'bʊr]
course, dish	rett (m)	['rɛt]
to order (meal)	å bestille	[ɔ be'stilə]
to make an order	å bestille	[ɔ be'stilə]
aperitif	aperitiff (m)	[ɑperi'tif]
starter	forrett (m)	['fɔrɛt]
dessert, pudding	dessert (m)	[de'sɛːr]
bill	regning (m/f)	['rɛjniŋ]
to pay the bill	å betale regningen	[ɔ be'tɑlə 'rɛjniŋən]
to give change	å gi tilbake veksel	[ɔ ji til'bɑkə 'vɛksəl]
tip	driks (m)	['driks]

50. Meals

food	mat (m)	['mɑt]
to eat (vi, vt)	å spise	[ɔ 'spisə]

breakfast	frokost (m)	['frʊkɔst]
to have breakfast	å spise frokost	[ɔ 'spisə ˌfrʊkɔst]
lunch	lunsj, lunch (m)	['lʉnʂ]
to have lunch	å spise lunsj	[ɔ 'spisə ˌlʉnʂ]
dinner	middag (m)	['miˌda]
to have dinner	å spise middag	[ɔ 'spisə 'miˌda]

appetite	appetitt (m)	[ape'tit]
Enjoy your meal!	God appetitt!	['gʊ ape'tit]

to open (~ a bottle)	å åpne	[ɔ 'ɔpnə]
to spill (liquid)	å spille	[ɔ 'spilə]
to spill out (vi)	å bli spilt	[ɔ 'bli 'spilt]

to boil (vi)	å koke	[ɔ 'kʊkə]
to boil (vt)	å koke	[ɔ 'kʊkə]
boiled (~ water)	kokt	['kʊkt]
to chill, cool down (vt)	å svalne	[ɔ 'svalnə]
to chill (vi)	å avkjøles	[ɔ 'avˌçœləs]

taste, flavour	smak (m)	['smak]
aftertaste	bismak (m)	['bismak]

to slim down (lose weight)	å være på diet	[ɔ 'værə pɔ di'et]
diet	diett (m)	[di'et]
vitamin	vitamin (n)	[vita'min]
calorie	kalori (m)	[kalʉ'ri]
vegetarian (n)	vegetarianer (m)	[vegetari'anər]
vegetarian (adj)	vegetarisk	[vege'tarisk]

fats (nutrient)	fett (n)	['fɛt]
proteins	proteiner (n pl)	[prɔte'inər]
carbohydrates	kullhydrater (n pl)	['kʉlhyˌdratər]
slice (of lemon, ham)	skive (m/f)	['ʂivə]
piece (of cake, pie)	stykke (n)	['stʏkə]
crumb (of bread, cake, etc.)	smule (m)	['smʉlə]

51. Cooked dishes

course, dish	rett (m)	['rɛt]
cuisine	kjøkken (n)	['çœkən]
recipe	oppskrift (m)	['ɔpˌskrift]
portion	porsjon (m)	[pɔ'ʂʉn]

salad	salat (m)	[sa'lat]
soup	suppe (m/f)	['sʉpə]

clear soup (broth)	buljong (m)	[bu'ljɔŋ]
sandwich (bread)	smørbrød (n)	['smørˌbrø]
fried eggs	speilegg (n)	['spæjlˌɛg]

hamburger (beefburger)	hamburger (m)	['hambʊrgər]
beefsteak	biff (m)	['bif]
side dish	tilbehør (n)	['tilbəˌhør]

55

spaghetti	spagetti (m)	[spɑ'gɛti]
mash	potetmos (m)	[pʉ'tet͵mʉs]
pizza	pizza (m)	['pitsɑ]
porridge (oatmeal, etc.)	grøt (m)	['grøt]
omelette	omelett (m)	[ɔmə'let]

boiled (e.g. ~ beef)	kokt	['kʉkt]
smoked (adj)	røkt	['røkt]
fried (adj)	stekt	['stɛkt]
dried (adj)	tørket	['tœrkət]
frozen (adj)	frossen, dypfryst	['frɔsən], ['dyp͵frʏst]
pickled (adj)	syltet	['sʏltət]

sweet (sugary)	søt	['søt]
salty (adj)	salt	['sɑlt]
cold (adj)	kald	['kɑl]
hot (adj)	het, varm	['het], ['vɑrm]
bitter (adj)	bitter	['bitər]
tasty (adj)	lekker	['lekər]

to cook in boiling water	å koke	[ɔ 'kʉkə]
to cook (dinner)	å lage	[ɔ 'lagə]
to fry (vt)	å steke	[ɔ 'stekə]
to heat up (food)	å varme opp	[ɔ 'vɑrmə ɔp]

to salt (vt)	å salte	[ɔ 'sɑltə]
to pepper (vt)	å pepre	[ɔ 'pɛprə]
to grate (vt)	å rive	[ɔ 'rivə]
peel (n)	skall (n)	['skɑl]
to peel (vt)	å skrelle	[ɔ 'skrɛlə]

52. Food

meat	kjøtt (n)	['çœt]
chicken	høne (m/f)	['hønə]
poussin	kylling (m)	['çyliŋ]
duck	and (m/f)	['ɑn]
goose	gås (m/f)	['gɔs]
game	vilt (n)	['vilt]
turkey	kalkun (m)	[kɑl'kʉn]

pork	svinekjøtt (n)	['svinə͵çœt]
veal	kalvekjøtt (n)	['kɑlvə͵çœt]
lamb	fårekjøtt (n)	['foːrə͵çœt]
beef	oksekjøtt (n)	['ɔksə͵çœt]
rabbit	kanin (m)	[kɑ'nin]

sausage (bologna, pepperoni, etc.)	pølse (m/f)	['pølsə]
vienna sausage (frankfurter)	wienerpølse (m/f)	['vinər͵pølsə]
bacon	bacon (n)	['bɛjkən]
ham	skinke (m)	['ʂinkə]
gammon	skinke (m)	['ʂinkə]
pâté	pate, paté (m)	[pɑ'te]

liver	lever (m)	['levər]
mince (minced meat)	kjøttfarse (m)	['çœt͡farʂə]
tongue	tunge (m/f)	['tʉŋə]

egg	egg (n)	['ɛg]
eggs	egg (n pl)	['ɛg]
egg white	eggehvite (m)	['ɛgə͜vitə]
egg yolk	plomme (m/f)	['plʊmə]

fish	fisk (m)	['fisk]
seafood	sjømat (m)	['ʂø͜mat]
crustaceans	krepsdyr (n pl)	['krɛps͜dyr]
caviar	kaviar (m)	['kavi͜ar]

crab	krabbe (m)	['krabə]
prawn	reke (m/f)	['rekə]
oyster	østers (m)	['østəʂ]
spiny lobster	langust (m)	[laŋ'gʉst]
octopus	blekksprut (m)	['blek͜sprʉt]
squid	blekksprut (m)	['blek͜sprʉt]

sturgeon	stør (m)	['stør]
salmon	laks (m)	['laks]
halibut	kveite (m/f)	['kvæjtə]

cod	torsk (m)	['toʂk]
mackerel	makrell (m)	[ma'krɛl]
tuna	tunfisk (m)	['tʉn͜fisk]
eel	ål (m)	['ɔl]

trout	ørret (m)	['øret]
sardine	sardin (m)	[sɑ:'d̦in]
pike	gjedde (m/f)	['jɛdə]
herring	sild (m/f)	['sil]

bread	brød (n)	['brø]
cheese	ost (m)	['ʊst]
sugar	sukker (n)	['sʉkər]
salt	salt (n)	['salt]
rice	ris (m)	['ris]
pasta (macaroni)	pasta, makaroni (m)	['pasta], [maka'rʊni]
noodles	nudler (m pl)	['nʉdlər]

butter	smør (n)	['smør]
vegetable oil	vegetabilsk olje (m)	[vegeta'bilsk ͵ɔljə]
sunflower oil	solsikkeolje (m)	['sʊlsikə͵ɔljə]
margarine	margarin (m)	[marga'rin]

| olives | olivener (m pl) | [ʊ'livenər] |
| olive oil | olivenolje (m) | [ʊ'livən͵ɔljə] |

milk	melk (m/f)	['mɛlk]
condensed milk	kondensert melk (m/f)	[kʊndən'se:t ͵mɛlk]
yogurt	jogurt (m)	['jɔgʉ:t]
soured cream	rømme, syrnet fløte (m)	['rœmə], ['sy:ɳet 'fløtə]
cream (of milk)	fløte (m)	['fløtə]

| mayonnaise | majones (m) | [majɔ'nɛs] |
| buttercream | krem (m) | ['krɛm] |

cereal grains (wheat, etc.)	gryn (n)	['gryn]
flour	mel (n)	['mel]
tinned food	hermetikk (m)	[hɛrme'tik]

cornflakes	cornflakes (m)	['kɔːɳˌflejks]
honey	honning (m)	['hɔniŋ]
jam	syltetøy (n)	['syltəˌtøj]
chewing gum	tyggegummi (m)	['tygəˌgʉmi]

53. Drinks

water	vann (n)	['van]
drinking water	drikkevann (n)	['drikəˌvan]
mineral water	mineralvann (n)	[minə'ralˌvan]

still (adj)	uten kullsyre	['ʉtən kʉl'syrə]
carbonated (adj)	kullsyret	[kʉl'syrət]
sparkling (adj)	med kullsyre	[me kʉl'syrə]
ice	is (m)	['is]
with ice	med is	[me 'is]

non-alcoholic (adj)	alkoholfri	['alkʉhʉlˌfri]
soft drink	alkoholfri drikk (m)	['alkʉhʉlˌfri drik]
refreshing drink	leskedrikk (m)	['leskəˌdrik]
lemonade	limonade (m)	[limɔ'nadə]

spirits	rusdrikker (m pl)	['rʉsˌdrikər]
wine	vin (m)	['vin]
white wine	hvitvin (m)	['vitˌvin]
red wine	rødvin (m)	['røˌvin]

liqueur	likør (m)	[li'kør]
champagne	champagne (m)	[ʂam'panjə]
vermouth	vermut (m)	['værmʉt]

whisky	whisky (m)	['viski]
vodka	vodka (m)	['vɔdka]
gin	gin (m)	['dʒin]
cognac	konjakk (m)	['kʉnjak]
rum	rom (m)	['rʉm]

coffee	kaffe (m)	['kafə]
black coffee	svart kaffe (m)	['svaːt 'kafə]
white coffee	kaffe (m) med melk	['kafə me 'mɛlk]
cappuccino	cappuccino (m)	[kapʉ'tʃinɔ]
instant coffee	pulverkaffe (m)	['pʉlvərˌkafə]

milk	melk (m/f)	['mɛlk]
cocktail	cocktail (m)	['kɔkˌtɛjl]
milkshake	milkshake (m)	['milkˌʂɛjk]
juice	jus, juice (m)	['dʒʉs]

tomato juice	tomatjuice (m)	[tʊ'mat,dʒʉs]
orange juice	appelsinjuice (m)	[apel'sin,dʒʉs]
freshly squeezed juice	nypresset juice (m)	['ny,prɛsə 'dʒʉs]

beer	øl (m/n)	['øl]
lager	lettøl (n)	['let,øl]
bitter	mørkt øl (n)	['mœrkt,øl]

tea	te (m)	['te]
black tea	svart te (m)	['svɑːʈ ,te]
green tea	grønn te (m)	['grœn ,te]

54. Vegetables

| vegetables | grønnsaker (m pl) | ['grœn,sɑkər] |
| greens | grønnsaker (m pl) | ['grœn,sɑkər] |

tomato	tomat (m)	[tʊ'mat]
cucumber	agurk (m)	[a'gʉrk]
carrot	gulrot (m/f)	['gʉl,rʊt]
potato	potet (m/f)	[pʊ'tet]
onion	løk (m)	['løk]
garlic	hvitløk (m)	['vit,løk]

| cabbage | kål (m) | ['kɔl] |
| cauliflower | blomkål (m) | ['blɔm,kɔl] |

| Brussels sprouts | rosenkål (m) | ['rʊsən,kɔl] |
| broccoli | brokkoli (m) | ['brɔkoli] |

beetroot	rødbete (m/f)	['rø,betə]
aubergine	aubergine (m)	[ɔbɛr'ʂin]
courgette	squash (m)	['skvɔʂ]

| pumpkin | gresskar (n) | ['grɛskɑr] |
| turnip | nepe (m/f) | ['nepə] |

parsley	persille (m/f)	[pæ'ʂilə]
dill	dill (m)	['dil]
lettuce	salat (m)	[sa'lat]
celery	selleri (m/n)	[sɛle,ri]

| asparagus | asparges (m) | [a'sparʂəs] |
| spinach | spinat (m) | [spi'nat] |

| pea | erter (m pl) | ['æːtər] |
| beans | bønner (m/f pl) | ['bœnər] |

| maize | mais (m) | ['mais] |
| kidney bean | bønne (m/f) | ['bœnə] |

sweet paper	pepper (m)	['pɛpər]
radish	reddik (m)	['rɛdik]
artichoke	artisjokk (m)	[,aːʈi'ʂɔk]

55. Fruits. Nuts

fruit	frukt (m/f)	['frʉkt]
apple	eple (n)	['ɛplə]
pear	pære (m/f)	['pærə]
lemon	sitron (m)	[si'trʊn]
orange	appelsin (m)	[ɑpel'sin]
strawberry (garden ~)	jordbær (n)	['juːr,bær]
tangerine	mandarin (m)	[mɑndɑ'rin]
plum	plomme (m/f)	['plʊmə]
peach	fersken (m)	['fæʂkən]
apricot	aprikos (m)	[ɑpri'kʊs]
raspberry	bringebær (n)	['briŋə,bær]
pineapple	ananas (m)	['ɑnɑnɑs]
banana	banan (m)	[bɑ'nɑn]
watermelon	vannmelon (m)	['vɑnme,lʊn]
grape	drue (m)	['drʉə]
sour cherry	kirsebær (n)	['çiʂə,bær]
sweet cherry	morell (m)	[mʊ'rɛl]
melon	melon (m)	[me'lun]
grapefruit	grapefrukt (m/f)	['grɛjp,frʉkt]
avocado	avokado (m)	[ɑvɔ'kadɔ]
papaya	papaya (m)	[pɑ'pɑja]
mango	mango (m)	['mɑŋu]
pomegranate	granateple (n)	[grɑ'nɑt,ɛplə]
redcurrant	rips (m)	['rips]
blackcurrant	solbær (n)	['sʊl,bær]
gooseberry	stikkelsbær (n)	['stikəls,bær]
bilberry	blåbær (n)	['blɔ,bær]
blackberry	bjørnebær (m)	['bjœːŋə,bær]
raisin	rosin (m)	[rʊ'sin]
fig	fiken (m)	['fikən]
date	daddel (m)	['dadəl]
peanut	jordnøtt (m)	['juːr,nœt]
almond	mandel (m)	['mɑndəl]
walnut	valnøtt (m/f)	['val,nœt]
hazelnut	hasselnøtt (m/f)	['hasəl,nœt]
coconut	kokosnøtt (m/f)	['kʊkʊs,nœt]
pistachios	pistasier (m pl)	[pi'stɑʂiər]

56. Bread. Sweets

bakers' confectionery (pastry)	bakevarer (m/f pl)	['bɑkə,varər]
bread	brød (n)	['brø]
biscuits	kjeks (m)	['çɛks]
chocolate (n)	sjokolade (m)	[ʂʊkʊ'lɑdə]
chocolate (as adj)	sjokolade-	[ʂʊkʊ'lɑdə-]

T&P Books. Theme-based dictionary British English-Norwegian - 3000 words

| granddaughter | barnebarn (n) | ['bɑːŋəˌbɑːn̩] |
| grandchildren | barnebarn (n pl) | ['bɑːŋəˌbɑːn̩] |

uncle	onkel (m)	['ʊnkəl]
aunt	tante (m/f)	['tɑntə]
nephew	nevø (m)	[ne'vø]
niece	niese (m/f)	[ni'esə]

mother-in-law (wife's mother)	svigermor (m/f)	['svigərˌmʊr]
father-in-law (husband's father)	svigerfar (m)	['svigərˌfɑr]
son-in-law (daughter's husband)	svigersønn (m)	['svigərˌsœn]
stepmother	stemor (m/f)	['steˌmʊr]
stepfather	stefar (m)	['steˌfɑr]

infant	brystbarn (n)	['brʏstˌbɑːn̩]
baby (infant)	spedbarn (n)	['speˌbɑːn̩]
little boy, kid	lite barn (n)	['litə 'bɑːn̩]

wife	kone (m/f)	['kʊnə]
husband	mann (m)	['mɑn]
spouse (husband)	ektemann (m)	['ɛktəˌmɑn]
spouse (wife)	hustru (m)	['hʉstrʉ]

married (masc.)	gift	['jift]
married (fem.)	gift	['jift]
single (unmarried)	ugift	[ʉːˈjift]
bachelor	ungkar (m)	['ʉŋˌkɑr]
divorced (masc.)	fraskilt	['frɑˌʂilt]
widow	enke (m)	['ɛnkə]
widower	enkemann (m)	['ɛnkəˌmɑn]

relative	slektning (m)	['ʂlektniŋ]
close relative	nær slektning (m)	['nær 'ʂlektniŋ]
distant relative	fjern slektning (m)	['fjæːn̩ 'ʂlektniŋ]
relatives	slektninger (m pl)	['ʂlektniŋər]

orphan (boy or girl)	foreldreløst barn (n)	[fɔrˈɛldrələst ˌbɑːn̩]
guardian (of a minor)	formynder (m)	['fɔrˌmʏnər]
to adopt (a boy)	å adoptere	[ɔ ɑdɔp'terə]
to adopt (a girl)	å adoptere	[ɔ ɑdɔp'terə]

60. Friends. Colleagues

friend (masc.)	venn (m)	['vɛn]
friend (fem.)	venninne (m/f)	[vɛ'ninə]
friendship	vennskap (n)	['vɛnˌskɑp]
to be friends	å være venner	[ɔ 'værə 'vɛnər]

pal (masc.)	venn (m)	['vɛn]
pal (fem.)	venninne (m/f)	[vɛ'ninə]
partner	partner (m)	['pɑːtnər]

63

chief (boss)	sjef (m)	['ʂɛf]
superior (n)	overordnet (m)	['ɔvərˌɔrdnet]
owner, proprietor	eier (m)	['æjər]
subordinate (n)	underordnet (m)	['ʉnərˌɔrdnet]
colleague	kollega (m)	[kʉ'lega]
acquaintance (person)	bekjent (m)	[be'çɛnt]
fellow traveller	medpassasjer (m)	['meˌpasa'sɛr]
classmate	klassekamerat (m)	['klasəˌkamə'rɑːt]
neighbour (masc.)	nabo (m)	['nɑbʉ]
neighbour (fem.)	nabo (m)	['nɑbʉ]
neighbours	naboer (m pl)	['nɑbʉər]

HUMAN BODY. MEDICINE

61. Head

head	hode (n)	['hʊdə]
face	ansikt (n)	['ansikt]
nose	nese (m/f)	['nesə]
mouth	munn (m)	['mʉn]

eye	øye (n)	['øjə]
eyes	øyne (n pl)	['øjnə]
pupil	pupil (m)	[pʉ'pil]
eyebrow	øyenbryn (n)	['øjən,bryn]
eyelash	øyenvipp (m)	['øjən,vip]
eyelid	øyelokk (m)	['øjə,lɔk]

tongue	tunge (m/f)	['tʉŋə]
tooth	tann (m/f)	['tan]
lips	lepper (m/f pl)	['lepər]
cheekbones	kinnbein (n pl)	['çin,bæjn]
gum	tannkjøtt (n)	['tan,çœt]
palate	gane (m)	['ganə]

nostrils	nesebor (n pl)	['nesə,bʊr]
chin	hake (m/f)	['hakə]
jaw	kjeve (m)	['çɛvə]
cheek	kinn (n)	['çin]

forehead	panne (m/f)	['panə]
temple	tinning (m)	['tiniŋ]
ear	øre (n)	['ørə]
back of the head	bakhode (n)	['bak,hodə]
neck	hals (m)	['hals]
throat	strupe, hals (m)	['strʉpə], ['hals]

hair	hår (n pl)	['hɔr]
hairstyle	frisyre (m)	[fri'syrə]
haircut	hårfasong (m)	['hoːrfɑ,sɔŋ]
wig	parykk (m)	[pa'rʏk]

moustache	mustasje (m)	[mʉ'staʃə]
beard	skjegg (n)	['ʂɛg]
to have (a beard, etc.)	å ha	[ɔ 'ha]
plait	flette (m/f)	['fletə]
sideboards	bakkenbarter (pl)	['bakən,baːʈər]

red-haired (adj)	rødhåret	['rø,hoːrət]
grey (hair)	grå	['grɔ]
bald (adj)	skallet	['skalət]
bald patch	skallet flekk (m)	['skalət ,flek]

| ponytail | hestehale (m) | ['hɛstə‚halə] |
| fringe | pannelugg (m) | ['panə‚lʉg] |

62. Human body

| hand | hånd (m/f) | ['hɔn] |
| arm | arm (m) | ['arm] |

finger	finger (m)	['fiŋər]
toe	tå (m/f)	['tɔ]
thumb	tommel (m)	['tɔməl]
little finger	lillefinger (m)	['lilə‚fiŋər]
nail	negl (m)	['nɛjl]

fist	knyttneve (m)	['knʏt‚nevə]
palm	håndflate (m/f)	['hɔn‚flatə]
wrist	håndledd (n)	['hɔn‚led]
forearm	underarm (m)	['ʉnər‚arm]
elbow	albue (m)	['al‚bʉə]
shoulder	skulder (m)	['skʉldər]

leg	bein (n)	['bæjn]
foot	fot (m)	['fʊt]
knee	kne (n)	['knɛ]
calf (part of leg)	legg (m)	['leg]
hip	hofte (m)	['hoftə]
heel	hæl (m)	['hæl]

body	kropp (m)	['krɔp]
stomach	mage (m)	['magə]
chest	bryst (n)	['brʏst]
breast	bryst (n)	['brʏst]
flank	side (m/f)	['sidə]
back	rygg (m)	['rʏg]
lower back	korsrygg (m)	['kɔ:‚ʂ‚rʏg]
waist	liv (n), midje (m/f)	['liv], ['midjə]

navel (belly button)	navle (m)	['navlə]
buttocks	rumpeballer (m pl)	['rʉmpə‚balər]
bottom	bak (m)	['bak]

beauty spot	føflekk (m)	['fø‚flek]
birthmark (café au lait spot)	fødselsmerke (n)	['føtsəls‚mærke]
tattoo	tatovering (m/f)	[tatʉ'vɛriŋ]
scar	arr (n)	['ar]

63. Diseases

illness	sykdom (m)	['sʏk‚dɔm]
to be ill	å være syk	[ɔ 'værə 'syk]
health	helse (m/f)	['hɛlsə]
runny nose (coryza)	snue (m)	['snʉə]

tonsillitis	angina (m)	[an'gina]
cold (illness)	forkjølelse (m)	[fɔr'çœləlsə]
to catch a cold	å forkjøle seg	[ɔ fɔr'çœlə sæj]

bronchitis	bronkitt (m)	[brɔn'kit]
pneumonia	lungebetennelse (m)	['luŋə be'tɛnəlsə]
flu, influenza	influensa (m)	[inflʉ'ɛnsa]

shortsighted (adj)	nærsynt	['næ,sʏnt]
longsighted (adj)	langsynt	['laŋsʏnt]
strabismus (crossed eyes)	skjeløydhet (m)	['ʂɛløjd,het]
squint-eyed (adj)	skjeløyd	['ʂɛl,øjd]
cataract	grå stær, katarakt (m)	['grɔ ,stær], [kata'rakt]
glaucoma	glaukom (n)	[glaʊ'kɔm]

stroke	hjerneslag (n)	['jæ:ŋə,slag]
heart attack	infarkt (n)	[in'farkt]
myocardial infarction	myokardieinfarkt (n)	['miɔ'kardiə in'farkt]
paralysis	paralyse, lammelse (m)	['para'lyse], ['laməlsə]
to paralyse (vt)	å lamme	[ɔ 'lamə]

allergy	allergi (m)	[alæ:'gi]
asthma	astma (m)	['astma]
diabetes	diabetes (m)	[dia'betəs]

| toothache | tannpine (m/f) | ['tan,pinə] |
| caries | karies (m) | ['karies] |

diarrhoea	diaré (m)	[dia'rɛ]
constipation	forstoppelse (m)	[fɔ'ʂtɔpəlsə]
stomach upset	magebesvær (m)	['magə,be'svær]
food poisoning	matforgiftning (m/f)	['mat,fɔr'jiftniŋ]
to get food poisoning	å få matforgiftning	[ɔ 'fɔ mat,fɔr'jiftniŋ]

arthritis	artritt (m)	[a:t'rit]
rickets	rakitt (m)	[ra'kit]
rheumatism	revmatisme (m)	[revma'tismə]
atherosclerosis	arteriosklerose (m)	[a:'teriʉskle,rʉsə]

gastritis	magekatarr, gastritt (m)	['magəka,tar], [,ga'strit]
appendicitis	appendisitt (m)	[apɛndi'sit]
cholecystitis	galleblærebetennelse (m)	['galə,blærə be'tɛnəlsə]
ulcer	magesår (n)	['magə,sɔr]

measles	meslinger (m pl)	['mɛs,liŋər]
rubella (German measles)	røde hunder (m pl)	['røde 'hʉnər]
jaundice	gulsott (m/f)	['gʉl,sʊt]
hepatitis	hepatitt (m)	[hepa'tit]

schizophrenia	schizofreni (m)	[ʂisʉfre'ni]
rabies (hydrophobia)	rabies (m)	['rabies]
neurosis	nevrose (m)	[nev'rʉsə]
concussion	hjernerystelse (m)	['jæ:ŋə,rʏstəlsə]

| cancer | kreft, cancer (m) | ['krɛft], ['kansər] |
| sclerosis | sklerose (m) | [skle'rʉsə] |

multiple sclerosis	multippel sklerose (m)	[muɫ'tipəl skle'rʊsə]
alcoholism	alkoholisme (m)	[alkʊhʊ'lismə]
alcoholic (n)	alkoholiker (m)	[alkʊ'hʊlikər]
syphilis	syfilis (m)	['syfilis]
AIDS	AIDS, aids (m)	['ɛjds]

tumour	svulst, tumor (m)	['svuɫst], [tu'mʊr]
malignant (adj)	ondartet, malign	['ʊn‚ɑ:ʈət], [mɑ'lign]
benign (adj)	godartet	['gʊ‚ɑ:ʈət]

fever	feber (m)	['febər]
malaria	malaria (m)	[mɑ'lɑria]
gangrene	koldbrann (m)	['kɔlbran]
seasickness	sjøsyke (m)	['ʃø‚sykə]
epilepsy	epilepsi (m)	[ɛpilep'si]

epidemic	epidemi (m)	[ɛpide'mi]
typhus	tyfus (m)	['tyfus]
tuberculosis	tuberkulose (m)	[tubærkʊ'lɔsə]
cholera	kolera (m)	['kʊlera]
plague (bubonic ~)	pest (m)	['pɛst]

64. Symptoms. Treatments. Part 1

symptom	symptom (n)	[symp'tum]
temperature	temperatur (m)	[tɛmpəra'tur]
high temperature (fever)	høy temperatur (m)	['høj tɛmpəra'tur]
pulse	puls (m)	['puls]

dizziness (vertigo)	svimmelhet (m)	['svimәl‚het]
hot (adj)	varm	['vɑrm]
shivering	skjelving (m/f)	['ʃɛlviŋ]
pale (e.g. ~ face)	blek	['blek]

cough	hoste (m)	['hʊstə]
to cough (vi)	å hoste	[ɔ 'hʊstə]
to sneeze (vi)	å nyse	[ɔ 'nysə]
faint	besvimelse (m)	[bɛ'svimәlsə]
to faint (vi)	å besvime	[ɔ be'svimə]

bruise (hématome)	blåmerke (n)	['blɔ‚mærkə]
bump (lump)	bule (m)	['buɫə]
to bang (bump)	å slå seg	[ɔ 'sɫɔ sæj]
contusion (bruise)	blåmerke (n)	['blɔ‚mærkə]
to get a bruise	å slå seg	[ɔ 'sɫɔ sæj]

to limp (vi)	å halte	[ɔ 'haltə]
dislocation	forvridning (m)	[fɔr'vridniŋ]
to dislocate (vt)	å forvri	[ɔ fɔr'vri]
fracture	brudd (n), fraktur (m)	['brud], [frak'tur]
to have a fracture	å få brudd	[ɔ 'fɔ 'brud]

| cut (e.g. paper ~) | skjæresår (n) | ['ʃæ:rə‚sɔr] |
| to cut oneself | å skjære seg | [ɔ 'ʃæ:rə sæj] |

bleeding	blødning (m/f)	['blødniŋ]
burn (injury)	brannsår (n)	['branˌsɔr]
to get burned	å brenne seg	[ɔ 'brɛnə sæj]

to prick (vt)	å stikke	[ɔ 'stikə]
to prick oneself	å stikke seg	[ɔ 'stikə sæj]
to injure (vt)	å skade	[ɔ 'skadə]
injury	skade (n)	['skadə]
wound	sår (n)	['sɔr]
trauma	traume (m)	['traʊmə]

to be delirious	å snakke i villelse	[ɔ 'snakə i 'viləlsə]
to stutter (vi)	å stamme	[ɔ 'stamə]
sunstroke	solstikk (n)	['sʊlˌstik]

65. Symptoms. Treatments. Part 2

pain, ache	smerte (m)	['smæːʈə]
splinter (in foot, etc.)	flis (m/f)	['flis]

sweat (perspiration)	svette (m)	['svɛtə]
to sweat (perspire)	å svette	[ɔ 'svɛtə]
vomiting	oppkast (n)	['ɔpˌkast]
convulsions	kramper (m pl)	['krampər]

pregnant (adj)	gravid	[gra'vid]
to be born	å fødes	[ɔ 'fødə]
delivery, labour	fødsel (m)	['føtsəl]
to deliver (~ a baby)	å føde	[ɔ 'fødə]
abortion	abort (m)	[a'bɔːʈ]

breathing, respiration	åndedrett (n)	['ɔndəˌdrɛt]
in-breath (inhalation)	innånding (m/f)	['inˌɔniŋ]
out-breath (exhalation)	utånding (m/f)	['ʉtˌɔndiŋ]
to exhale (breathe out)	å puste ut	[ɔ 'pʉstə ʉt]
to inhale (vi)	å ånde inn	[ɔ 'ɔndə ˌin]

disabled person	handikappet person (m)	['handiˌkapət pæ'ʂʉn]
cripple	krøpling (m)	['krøpliŋ]
drug addict	narkoman (m)	[narkʉ'man]

deaf (adj)	døv	['døv]
mute (adj)	stum	['stʉm]
deaf mute (adj)	døvstum	['døfˌstʉm]

mad, insane (adj)	gal	['gal]
madman (demented person)	gal mann (m)	['gal ˌman]
madwoman	gal kvinne (m/f)	['gal ˌkvinə]
to go insane	å bli sinnssyk	[ɔ 'bli 'sinˌsyk]

gene	gen (m)	['gen]
immunity	immunitet (m)	[imʉni'tet]
hereditary (adj)	arvelig	['arvəli]

congenital (adj)	medfødt	['me:ˌføt]
virus	virus (m)	['virʉs]
microbe	mikrobe (m)	[mi'krʉbə]
bacterium	bakterie (m)	[bak'teriə]
infection	infeksjon (m)	[infɛk'ʂʉn]

66. Symptoms. Treatments. Part 3

| hospital | sykehus (n) | ['sykəˌhʉs] |
| patient | pasient (m) | [pasi'ɛnt] |

diagnosis	diagnose (m)	[dia'gnʉsə]
cure	kur (m)	['kʉr]
medical treatment	behandling (m/f)	[be'handliŋ]
to get treatment	å bli behandlet	[ɔ 'bli be'handlət]
to treat (~ a patient)	å behandle	[ɔ be'handlə]
to nurse (look after)	å skjøtte	[ɔ 'ʂøtə]
care (nursing ~)	sykepleie (m/f)	['sykəˌplæjə]

operation, surgery	operasjon (m)	[ɔpəra'ʂʉn]
to bandage (head, limb)	å forbinde	[ɔ for'binə]
bandaging	forbinding (m)	[for'biniŋ]

vaccination	vaksinering (m/f)	[vaksi'neriŋ]
to vaccinate (vt)	å vaksinere	[ɔ vaksi'nerə]
injection	injeksjon (m), sprøyte (m/f)	[injɛk'ʂʉn], ['sprøjtə]
to give an injection	å gi en sprøyte	[ɔ 'ji en 'sprøjtə]

attack	anfall (n)	['anˌfal]
amputation	amputasjon (m)	[ampʉta'ʂʉn]
to amputate (vt)	å amputere	[ɔ ampʉ'terə]
coma	koma (m)	['kʉma]
to be in a coma	å ligge i koma	[ɔ 'ligə i 'kʉma]
intensive care	intensivavdeling (m/f)	['intenˌsiv 'avˌdeliŋ]

to recover (~ from flu)	å bli frisk	[ɔ 'bli 'frisk]
condition (patient's ~)	tilstand (m)	['tilˌstan]
consciousness	bevissthet (m)	[be'vistˌhet]
memory (faculty)	minne (n), hukommelse (m)	['minə], [hʉ'kɔməlsə]

to pull out (tooth)	å trekke ut	[ɔ 'trɛkə ʉt]
filling	fylling (m/f)	['fʏliŋ]
to fill (a tooth)	å plombere	[ɔ plʉm'berə]

| hypnosis | hypnose (m) | [hʏp'nʉsə] |
| to hypnotize (vt) | å hypnotisere | [ɔ hʏpnʉti'serə] |

67. Medicine. Drugs. Accessories

medicine, drug	medisin (m)	[medi'sin]
remedy	middel (n)	['midəl]
to prescribe (vt)	å ordinere	[ɔ ɔrdi'nerə]

prescription	resept (m)	[re'sɛpt]
tablet, pill	tablett (m)	[tab'let]
ointment	salve (m/f)	['sɑlvə]
ampoule	ampulle (m)	[ɑm'pʉlə]
mixture	mikstur (m)	[miks'tʉr]
syrup	sirup (m)	['sirʉp]
pill	pille (m/f)	['pilə]
powder	pulver (n)	['pʉlvər]

gauze bandage	gasbind (n)	['gɑs,bin]
cotton wool	vatt (m/n)	['vat]
iodine	jod (m/n)	['ʉd]

plaster	plaster (n)	['plɑstər]
eyedropper	pipette (m)	[pi'pɛtə]
thermometer	termometer (n)	[tɛrmʉ'metər]
syringe	sprøyte (m/f)	['sprøjtə]

| wheelchair | rullestol (m) | ['rʉlə,stʊl] |
| crutches | krykker (m/f pl) | ['krʏkər] |

painkiller	smertestillende middel (n)	['smæ:ʈə,stilenə 'midəl]
laxative	laksativ (n)	[lɑksa'tiv]
spirits (ethanol)	sprit (m)	['sprit]
medicinal herbs	legeurter (m/f pl)	['legə,ʉ:tər]
herbal (~ tea)	urte-	['ʉ:ʈə-]

FLAT

68. Flat

flat	leilighet (m/f)	['læjli‚het]
room	rom (n)	['rʊm]
bedroom	soverom (n)	['sɔvə‚rʊm]
dining room	spisestue (m/f)	['spisə‚stʉə]
living room	dagligstue (m/f)	['dagli‚stʉə]
study (home office)	arbeidsrom (n)	['arbæjds‚rʊm]
entry room	entré (m)	[ɑn'trɛ:]
bathroom	bad, baderom (n)	['bad], ['badə‚rʊm]
water closet	toalett, WC (n)	[tʊɑ'let], [vɛ'sɛ]
ceiling	tak (n)	['tak]
floor	gulv (n)	['gʉlv]
corner	hjørne (n)	['jœ:ŋə]

69. Furniture. Interior

furniture	møbler (n pl)	['møblər]
table	bord (n)	['bʊr]
chair	stol (m)	['stʊl]
bed	seng (m/f)	['sɛŋ]
sofa, settee	sofa (m)	['sʊfa]
armchair	lenestol (m)	['lenə‚stʊl]
bookcase	bokskap (n)	['bʊk‚skap]
shelf	hylle (m/f)	['hʏlə]
wardrobe	klesskap (n)	['kle‚skap]
coat rack (wall-mounted ~)	knaggbrett (n)	['knag‚brɛt]
coat stand	stumtjener (m)	['stʉm‚tjenər]
chest of drawers	kommode (m)	[kʊ'mʉdə]
coffee table	kaffebord (n)	['kafə‚bʊr]
mirror	speil (n)	['spæjl]
carpet	teppe (n)	['tɛpə]
small carpet	lite teppe (n)	['litə 'tɛpə]
fireplace	peis (m), ildsted (n)	['pæjs], ['ilsted]
candle	lys (n)	['lys]
candlestick	lysestake (m)	['lysə‚stakə]
drapes	gardiner (m/f pl)	[ga:'ɖinər]
wallpaper	tapet (n)	[ta'pet]

blinds (jalousie)	persienne (m)	[pæʂiˈenə]
table lamp	bordlampe (m/f)	[ˈbuɾˌlampə]
wall lamp (sconce)	vegglampe (m/f)	[ˈvɛgˌlampə]
standard lamp	gulvlampe (m/f)	[ˈgɵlvˌlampə]
chandelier	lysekrone (m/f)	[ˈlysəˌkrunə]
leg (of chair, table)	bein (n)	[ˈbæjn]
armrest	armlene (n)	[ˈarmˌlenə]
back (backrest)	rygg (m)	[ˈrʏg]
drawer	skuff (m)	[ˈskɵf]

70. Bedding

bedclothes	sengetøy (n)	[ˈsɛŋəˌtøj]
pillow	pute (m/f)	[ˈpɵtə]
pillowslip	putevar, putetrekk (n)	[ˈpɵtəˌvar], [ˈpɵtəˌtrɛk]
duvet	dyne (m/f)	[ˈdynə]
sheet	laken (n)	[ˈlakən]
bedspread	sengeteppe (n)	[ˈsɛŋəˌtɛpə]

71. Kitchen

kitchen	kjøkken (n)	[ˈçœkən]
gas	gass (m)	[ˈgas]
gas cooker	gasskomfyr (m)	[ˈgas kɔmˌfyr]
electric cooker	elektrisk komfyr (m)	[ɛˈlektrisk kɔmˌfyr]
oven	bakeovn (m)	[ˈbakəˌɔvn]
microwave oven	mikrobølgeovn (m)	[ˈmikrʉˌbølgəˈɔvn]
refrigerator	kjøleskap (n)	[ˈçœləˌskap]
freezer	fryser (m)	[ˈfrysər]
dishwasher	oppvaskmaskin (m)	[ˈɔpvask maˌʂin]
mincer	kjøttkvern (m/f)	[ˈçœtˌkveːŋ]
juicer	juicepresse (m/f)	[ˈdʒʉsˌprɛsə]
toaster	brødrister (m)	[ˈbrøˌristər]
mixer	mikser (m)	[ˈmiksər]
coffee machine	kaffetrakter (m)	[ˈkafəˌtraktər]
coffee pot	kaffekanne (m/f)	[ˈkafəˌkanə]
coffee grinder	kaffekvern (m/f)	[ˈkafəˌkveːŋ]
kettle	tekjele (m)	[ˈteˌçelə]
teapot	tekanne (m/f)	[ˈteˌkanə]
lid	lokk (n)	[ˈlɔk]
tea strainer	tesil (m)	[ˈteˌsil]
spoon	skje (m)	[ˈʂe]
teaspoon	teskje (m)	[ˈteˌʂe]
soup spoon	spiseskje (m)	[ˈspisəˌʂɛ]
fork	gaffel (m)	[ˈgafəl]
knife	kniv (m)	[ˈkniv]

tableware (dishes)	**servise** (n)	[sær'visə]
plate (dinner ~)	**tallerken** (m)	[ta'lærkən]
saucer	**tefat** (n)	['te͵fat]

shot glass	**shotglass** (n)	['ʂot͵glas]
glass (tumbler)	**glass** (n)	['glas]
cup	**kopp** (m)	['kɔp]

sugar bowl	**sukkerskål** (m/f)	['sʉkər͵skɔl]
salt cellar	**saltbøsse** (m/f)	['salt͵bøsə]
pepper pot	**pepperbøsse** (m/f)	['pɛpər͵bøsə]
butter dish	**smørkopp** (m)	['smœr͵kɔp]

stock pot (soup pot)	**gryte** (m/f)	['grytə]
frying pan (skillet)	**steikepanne** (m/f)	['stæjkə͵panə]
ladle	**sleiv** (m/f)	['ʂlæjv]
colander	**dørslag** (n)	['dœʂlag]
tray (serving ~)	**brett** (n)	['brɛt]

bottle	**flaske** (m)	['flaskə]
jar (glass)	**glasskrukke** (m/f)	['glas͵krʉkə]
tin (can)	**boks** (m)	['bɔks]

bottle opener	**flaskeåpner** (m)	['flaskə͵ɔpnər]
tin opener	**konservåpner** (m)	['kʉnsəv͵ɔpnər]
corkscrew	**korketrekker** (m)	['kɔrkə͵trɛkər]
filter	**filter** (n)	['filtər]
to filter (vt)	**å filtrere**	[ɔ fil'trerə]

waste (food ~, etc.)	**søppel** (m/f/n)	['sœpəl]
waste bin (kitchen ~)	**søppelbøtte** (m/f)	['sœpəl͵bœtə]

72. Bathroom

bathroom	**bad, baderom** (n)	['bad], ['badə͵rʊm]
water	**vann** (n)	['van]
tap	**kran** (m/f)	['kran]
hot water	**varmt vann** (n)	['varmt ͵van]
cold water	**kaldt vann** (n)	['kalt van]

toothpaste	**tannpasta** (m)	['tan͵pasta]
to clean one's teeth	**å pusse tennene**	[ɔ 'pʉsə 'tɛnənə]
toothbrush	**tannbørste** (m)	['tan͵bœʂtə]

to shave (vi)	**å barbere seg**	[ɔ bar'berə sæj]
shaving foam	**barberskum** (n)	[bar'bɛ͵skʉm]
razor	**høvel** (m)	['høvəl]

to wash (one's hands, etc.)	**å vaske**	[ɔ 'vaskə]
to have a bath	**å vaske seg**	[ɔ 'vaskə sæj]
shower	**dusj** (m)	['dʉʂ]
to have a shower	**å ta en dusj**	[ɔ 'ta en 'dʉʂ]
bath	**badekar** (n)	['badə͵kar]
toilet (toilet bowl)	**toalettstol** (m)	[tʊa'let͵stʊl]

sink (washbasin)	vaskeservant (m)	['vaskə‚sɛr'vant]
soap	såpe (m/f)	['soːpə]
soap dish	såpeskål (m/f)	['soːpə‚skɔl]

sponge	svamp (m)	['svamp]
shampoo	sjampo (m)	['ʂam‚pʊ]
towel	håndkle (n)	['hɔn‚klе]
bathrobe	badekåpe (m/f)	['badə‚koːpə]

laundry (process)	vask (m)	['vask]
washing machine	vaskemaskin (m)	['vaskə ma‚ʂin]
to do the laundry	å vaske tøy	[ɔ 'vaskə 'tøj]
washing powder	vaskepulver (n)	['vaskə‚pʉlvər]

73. Household appliances

TV, telly	TV (m), TV-apparat (n)	['tɛvɛ], ['tɛvɛ apa'rat]
tape recorder	båndopptaker (m)	['bɔn‚ɔptakər]
video	video (m)	['videʊ]
radio	radio (m)	['radiʊ]
player (CD, MP3, etc.)	spiller (m)	['spilər]

video projector	videoprojektor (m)	['videʊ prɔ'jɛktɔr]
home cinema	hjemmekino (m)	['jɛmə‚çinʊ]
DVD player	DVD-spiller (m)	[deve'de ‚spilər]
amplifier	forsterker (m)	[fo'ʂtærkər]
video game console	spillkonsoll (m)	['spil kʊn'sɔl]

video camera	videokamera (n)	['videʊ ‚kamera]
camera (photo)	kamera (n)	['kamera]
digital camera	digitalkamera (n)	[digi'tal ‚kamera]

vacuum cleaner	støvsuger (m)	['støf‚sʉgər]
iron (e.g. steam ~)	strykejern (n)	['strykə‚jæːn̩]
ironing board	strykebrett (n)	['strykə‚brɛt]

telephone	telefon (m)	[tele'fʊn]
mobile phone	mobiltelefon (m)	[mʊ'bil tele'fʊn]
typewriter	skrivemaskin (m)	['skrivə ma‚ʂin]
sewing machine	symaskin (m)	['siːma‚ʂin]

microphone	mikrofon (m)	[mikrʊ'fʊn]
headphones	hodetelefoner (n pl)	['hɔdetelə‚funər]
remote control (TV)	fjernkontroll (m)	['fjæːn̩ kʊn'trɔl]

CD, compact disc	CD-rom (m)	['sɛdɛ‚rʊm]
cassette, tape	kassett (m)	[ka'sɛt]
vinyl record	plate, skive (m/f)	['platə], ['ʂivə]

THE EARTH. WEATHER

74. Outer space

space	rommet, kosmos (n)	['rʊmə], ['kɔsmɔs]
space (as adj)	rom-	['rʊm-]
outer space	ytre rom (n)	['ytrə ˌrʊm]
world	verden (m)	['værdən]
universe	univers (n)	[ʉni'væʂ]
galaxy	galakse (m)	[ga'laksə]
star	stjerne (m/f)	['stjæːŋə]
constellation	stjernebilde (n)	['stjæːŋəˌbildə]
planet	planet (m)	[pla'net]
satellite	satellitt (m)	[satɛ'lit]
meteorite	meteoritt (m)	[meteʊ'rit]
comet	komet (m)	[kʊ'met]
asteroid	asteroide (n)	[asterʊ'idə]
orbit	bane (m)	['banə]
to revolve (~ around the Earth)	å rotere	[ɔ rɔ'terə]
atmosphere	atmosfære (m)	[atmʊ'sfærə]
the Sun	Solen	['sʊlən]
solar system	solsystem (n)	['sʊl sʏ'stem]
solar eclipse	solformørkelse (m)	['sʊl fɔr'mœrkəlsə]
the Earth	Jorden	['juːrən]
the Moon	Månen	['moːnən]
Mars	Mars	['maʂ]
Venus	Venus	['venʉs]
Jupiter	Jupiter	['jʉpitər]
Saturn	Saturn	['saˌtʉːŋ]
Mercury	Merkur	[mær'kʉr]
Uranus	Uranus	[ʉ'ranʉs]
Neptune	Neptun	[nɛp'tʉn]
Pluto	Pluto	['plʉtʊ]
Milky Way	Melkeveien	['mɛlkəˌvæjən]
Great Bear (Ursa Major)	den Store Bjørn	['dən 'stʉrə ˌbjœːn]
North Star	Nordstjernen, Polaris	['nuːrˌstjæːŋən], [pɔ'laris]
Martian	marsbeboer (m)	['maʂˌbebʊər]
extraterrestrial (n)	utenomjordisk vesen (n)	['ʉtənɔmˌjuːrdisk 'vesən]

alien	romvesen (n)	['rʊmˌvesən]
flying saucer	flygende tallerken (m)	['flygenə taˈlærkən]
spaceship	romskip (n)	['rʊmˌʂip]

| space station | romstasjon (m) | ['rʊmˌstaˈʂʊn] |
| blast-off | start (m), oppskyting (m/f) | ['stɑːt], ['ɔpˌʂytiŋ] |

engine	motor (m)	['mɔtʊr]
nozzle	dyse (m)	['dysə]
fuel	brensel (n), drivstoff (n)	['brɛnsəl], ['drifˌstɔf]

cockpit, flight deck	cockpit (m), flydekk (n)	['kɔkpit], ['flyˌdɛk]
aerial	antenne (m)	[anˈtɛnə]
porthole	koøye (n)	['kʊˌøjə]
solar panel	solbatteri (n)	['sʊl batɛ'ri]
spacesuit	romdrakt (m/f)	['rʊmˌdrɑkt]

| weightlessness | vektløshet (m/f) | ['vɛktløsˌhet] |
| oxygen | oksygen (n) | ['ɔksyˈgen] |

| docking (in space) | dokking (m/f) | ['dɔkiŋ] |
| to dock (vi, vt) | å dokke | [ɔ 'dɔkə] |

observatory	observatorium (n)	[ɔbsərvaˈtʊrium]
telescope	teleskop (n)	[teleˈskʊp]
to observe (vt)	å observere	[ɔ ɔbsɛrˈverə]
to explore (vt)	å utforske	[ɔ 'ʉtˌfɔʂkə]

75. The Earth

the Earth	Jorden	['juːrən]
the globe (the Earth)	jordklode (m)	['juːrˌklɔdə]
planet	planet (m)	[plaˈnet]

atmosphere	atmosfære (m)	[atmʊ'sfærə]
geography	geografi (m)	[geʊgraˈfi]
nature	natur (m)	[naˈtʉr]

globe (table ~)	globus (m)	['globʉs]
map	kart (n)	['kɑːt]
atlas	atlas (n)	['atlas]

| Europe | Europa | [ɛʉˈrʊpa] |
| Asia | Asia | ['asia] |

| Africa | Afrika | ['afrika] |
| Australia | Australia | [aʉ'stralia] |

America	Amerika	[a'merika]
North America	Nord-Amerika	['nʊːr a'merika]
South America	Sør-Amerika	['sør a'merika]

| Antarctica | Antarktis | [an'tarktis] |
| the Arctic | Arktis | ['arktis] |

76. Cardinal directions

north	nord (n)	['nuːr]
to the north	mot nord	[mʊt 'nuːr]
in the north	i nord	[i 'nuːr]
northern (adj)	nordlig	['nuːrli]
south	syd, sør	['syd], ['sør]
to the south	mot sør	[mʊt 'sør]
in the south	i sør	[i 'sør]
southern (adj)	sydlig, sørlig	['sydli], ['søː[i]
west	vest (m)	['vɛst]
to the west	mot vest	[mʊt 'vɛst]
in the west	i vest	[i 'vɛst]
western (adj)	vestlig, vest-	['vɛstli]
east	øst (m)	['øst]
to the east	mot øst	[mʊt 'øst]
in the east	i øst	[i 'øst]
eastern (adj)	østlig	['østli]

77. Sea. Ocean

sea	hav (n)	['hɑv]
ocean	verdenshav (n)	[værdəns'hɑv]
gulf (bay)	bukt (m/f)	['bʉkt]
straits	sund (n)	['sʉn]
land (solid ground)	fastland (n)	['fɑst,lɑn]
continent (mainland)	fastland, kontinent (n)	['fɑst,lɑn], [kʉnti'nɛnt]
island	øy (m/f)	['øj]
peninsula	halvøy (m/f)	['hɑl,øːj]
archipelago	skjærgård (m), arkipelag (n)	['şær,gɔr], [ɑrkipe'lɑg]
bay, cove	bukt (m/f)	['bʉkt]
harbour	havn (m/f)	['hɑvn]
lagoon	lagune (m)	[lɑ'gʉnə]
cape	nes (n), kapp (n)	['nes], ['kɑp]
atoll	atoll (m)	[ɑ'tɔl]
reef	rev (n)	['rev]
coral	korall (m)	[kʉ'rɑl]
coral reef	korallrev (n)	[kʉ'rɑl,rɛv]
deep (adj)	dyp	['dyp]
depth (deep water)	dybde (m)	['dʏbdə]
abyss	avgrunn (m)	['ɑv,grʉn]
trench (e.g. Mariana ~)	dyphavsgrop (m/f)	['dyphɑfs,grɔp]
current (Ocean ~)	strøm (m)	['strøm]
to surround (bathe)	å omgi	[ɔ 'ɔm,ji]
shore	kyst (m)	['çyst]

coast	kyst (m)	['çyst]
flow (flood tide)	flo (m/f)	['fluː]
ebb (ebb tide)	ebbe (m), fjære (m/f)	['ɛbə], ['fjærə]
shoal	sandbanke (m)	['san͵bankə]
bottom (~ of the sea)	bunn (m)	['bʉn]

wave	bølge (m)	['bølgə]
crest (~ of a wave)	bølgekam (m)	['bølgə͵kam]
spume (sea foam)	skum (n)	['skʉm]

storm (sea storm)	storm (m)	['storm]
hurricane	orkan (m)	[or'kan]
tsunami	tsunami (m)	[tsʉ'nɑmi]
calm (dead ~)	stille (m/f)	['stilə]
quiet, calm (adj)	stille	['stilə]

| pole | pol (m) | ['pʉl] |
| polar (adj) | pol-, polar | ['pʉl-], [pʉ'lɑr] |

latitude	bredde, latitude (m)	['brɛdə], ['lɑti͵tʉdə]
longitude	lengde (m/f)	['leŋdə]
parallel	breddegrad (m)	['brɛdə͵grɑd]
equator	ekvator (m)	[ɛ'kvɑtʉr]

sky	himmel (m)	['himəl]
horizon	horisont (m)	[hʉri'sont]
air	luft (f)	['lʉft]

lighthouse	fyr (n)	['fyr]
to dive (vi)	å dykke	[ɔ 'dʏkə]
to sink (ab. boat)	å synke	[ɔ 'sʏnkə]
treasures	skatter (m pl)	['skatər]

78. Seas & Oceans names

Atlantic Ocean	Atlanterhavet	[at'lantər͵have]
Indian Ocean	Indiahavet	['indiɑ͵have]
Pacific Ocean	Stillehavet	['stilə͵have]
Arctic Ocean	Polhavet	['pol͵have]

Black Sea	Svartehavet	['svɑː͵tə͵have]
Red Sea	Rødehavet	['rødə͵have]
Yellow Sea	Gulehavet	['gʉlə͵have]
White Sea	Kvitsjøen, Hvitehavet	['kvit͵søːn], ['vit͵have]

Caspian Sea	Kaspihavet	['kaspi͵have]
Dead Sea	Dødehavet	['dødə'have]
Mediterranean Sea	Middelhavet	['midəl͵have]

| Aegean Sea | Egeerhavet | [ɛ'geːər͵have] |
| Adriatic Sea | Adriahavet | ['adriɑ͵have] |

| Arabian Sea | Arabiahavet | [a'rabiɑ͵have] |
| Sea of Japan | Japanhavet | ['japan͵have] |

| Bering Sea | Beringhavet | ['beriŋˌhɑve] |
| South China Sea | Sør-Kina-havet | ['sørˌçinɑ 'hɑve] |

Coral Sea	Korallhavet	[kʊ'rɑlˌhɑve]
Tasman Sea	Tasmanhavet	[tɑs'manˌhɑve]
Caribbean Sea	Karibhavet	[kɑ'ribˌhɑve]

| Barents Sea | Barentshavet | ['bɑrɛnsˌhɑve] |
| Kara Sea | Karahavet | ['kɑrɑˌhɑve] |

North Sea	Nordsjøen	['nuːrˌ̥søːn]
Baltic Sea	Østersjøen	['østeˌ̥søːn]
Norwegian Sea	Norskehavet	['nɔ̥skeˌhɑve]

79. Mountains

mountain	fjell (n)	['fjɛl]
mountain range	fjellkjede (m)	['fjɛlˌçɛːdə]
mountain ridge	fjellrygg (m)	['fjɛlˌrʏg]

summit, top	topp (m)	['tɔp]
peak	tind (m)	['tin]
foot (~ of the mountain)	fot (m)	['fut]
slope (mountainside)	skråning (m)	['skrɔniŋ]

volcano	vulkan (m)	[vʉl'kɑn]
active volcano	virksom vulkan (m)	['virksɔm vʉl'kɑn]
dormant volcano	utslukt vulkan (m)	['ʉtˌslʉkt vʉl'kɑn]

eruption	utbrudd (n)	['ʉtˌbrʉd]
crater	krater (n)	['krɑtər]
magma	magma (m/n)	['mɑgmɑ]
lava	lava (m)	['lɑvɑ]
molten (~ lava)	glødende	['glødenə]

canyon	canyon (m)	['kɑnjən]
gorge	gjel (n), kløft (m)	['jel], ['klœft]
crevice	renne (m/f)	['rɛnə]
abyss (chasm)	avgrunn (m)	['ɑvˌgrʉn]

pass, col	pass (n)	['pɑs]
plateau	platå (n)	[plɑ'to]
cliff	klippe (m)	['klipə]
hill	ås (m)	['ɔs]

glacier	bre, jøkel (m)	['bre], ['jøkəl]
waterfall	foss (m)	['fɔs]
geyser	geysir (m)	['gɛjsir]
lake	innsjø (m)	['in'sø]

plain	slette (m/f)	['ʂletə]
landscape	landskap (n)	['lanˌskɑp]
echo	ekko (n)	['ɛkʊ]
alpinist	alpinist (m)	[ɑlpi'nist]

rock climber	fjellklatrer (m)	['fjɛlˌklatrər]
to conquer (in climbing)	å erobre	[ɔ ɛ'rʊbrə]
climb (an easy ~)	bestigning (m/f)	[be'stigniŋ]

80. Mountains names

The Alps	Alpene	['alpenə]
Mont Blanc	Mont Blanc	[ˌmɔn'blan]
The Pyrenees	Pyreneene	[pyre'neːənə]

The Carpathians	Karpatene	[kar'patenə]
The Ural Mountains	Uralfjellene	[ʉ'ral ˌfjɛlenə]
The Caucasus Mountains	Kaukasus	['kaʊkasʉs]
Mount Elbrus	Elbrus	[ɛl'brʉs]

The Altai Mountains	Altaj	[al'taj]
The Tian Shan	Tien Shan	[ti'enˌsan]
The Pamir Mountains	Pamir	[pa'mir]
The Himalayas	Himalaya	[hima'laja]
Mount Everest	Everest	['ɛve'rɛst]

| The Andes | Andes | ['andəs] |
| Mount Kilimanjaro | Kilimanjaro | [kiliman'dʂarʊ] |

81. Rivers

river	elv (m/f)	['ɛlv]
spring (natural source)	kilde (m)	['çildə]
riverbed (river channel)	elveleie (n)	['ɛlvəˌlæje]
basin (river valley)	flodbasseng (n)	['flʊd baˌseŋ]
to flow into ...	å munne ut ...	[ɔ 'mʉnə ʉt ...]

| tributary | bielv (m/f) | ['biˌelv] |
| bank (of river) | bredd (m) | ['brɛd] |

current (stream)	strøm (m)	['strøm]
downstream (adv)	medstrøms	['meˌstrøms]
upstream (adv)	motstrøms	['mʊtˌstrøms]

inundation	oversvømmelse (m)	['ɔvəˌsvœmelsə]
flooding	flom (m)	['flɔm]
to overflow (vi)	å overflø	[ɔ 'ɔvərˌflø]
to flood (vt)	å oversvømme	[ɔ 'ɔvəˌsvœmə]

| shallow (shoal) | grunne (m/f) | ['grʉnə] |
| rapids | stryk (m/n) | ['stryk] |

dam	demning (m)	['dɛmniŋ]
canal	kanal (m)	[ka'nal]
reservoir (artificial lake)	reservoar (n)	[resɛrvʊ'ar]
sluice, lock	sluse (m)	['ʂlʉsə]
water body (pond, etc.)	vannmasse (m)	['vanˌmasə]

swamp (marshland)	myr, sump (m)	['myr], ['sump]
bog, marsh	hengemyr (m)	['hɛŋəˌmyr]
whirlpool	virvel (m)	['virvəl]

stream (brook)	bekk (m)	['bɛk]
drinking (ab. water)	drikke-	['drikə-]
fresh (~ water)	fersk-	['fæʂk-]

ice	is (m)	['is]
to freeze over (ab. river, etc.)	å fryse til	[ɔ 'frysə til]

82. Rivers names

Seine	Seine	['sɛːn]
Loire	Loire	[lu'ɑːr]

Thames	Themsen	['tɛmsən]
Rhine	Rhinen	['riːnən]
Danube	Donau	['dɔnaʊ]

Volga	Volga	['vɔlgɑ]
Don	Don	['dɔn]
Lena	Lena	['lenɑ]

Yellow River	Huang He	[ˌhwɑn'hɛ]
Yangtze	Yangtze	['jaŋtse]
Mekong	Mekong	[me'kɔŋ]
Ganges	Ganges	['gaŋes]

Nile River	Nilen	['nilən]
Congo River	Kongo	['kɔŋgʊ]
Okavango River	Okavango	[ʊkɑ'vɑngʊ]
Zambezi River	Zambezi	[sɑm'besi]
Limpopo River	Limpopo	[limpo'pɔ]
Mississippi River	Mississippi	['misi'sipi]

83. Forest

forest, wood	skog (m)	['skʊg]
forest (as adj)	skog-	['skʊg-]

thick forest	tett skog (n)	['tɛt ˌskʊg]
grove	lund (m)	['lʉn]
forest clearing	glenne (m/f)	['glenə]

thicket	krattskog (m)	['kratˌskʊg]
scrubland	kratt (n)	['krat]

footpath (troddenpath)	sti (m)	['sti]
gully	ravine (m)	[rɑ'vinə]
tree	tre (n)	['trɛ]
leaf	blad (n)	['blɑ]

leaves (foliage)	løv (n)	['løv]
fall of leaves	løvfall (n)	['løv,fal]
to fall (ab. leaves)	å falle	[ɔ 'falə]
top (of the tree)	tretopp (m)	['trɛ,tɔp]

branch	kvist, gren (m)	['kvist], ['gren]
bough	gren, grein (m/f)	['gren], ['græjn]
bud (on shrub, tree)	knopp (m)	['knɔp]
needle (of pine tree)	nål (m/f)	['nɔl]
fir cone	kongle (m/f)	['kʊŋlə]

hollow (in a tree)	trehull (n)	['trɛ,hʉl]
nest	reir (n)	['ræjr]
burrow (animal hole)	hule (m/f)	['hʉlə]

trunk	stamme (m)	['stamə]
root	rot (m/f)	['rʊt]
bark	bark (m)	['bark]
moss	mose (m)	['mʊsə]

to uproot (remove trees or tree stumps)	å rykke opp med roten	[ɔ 'rʏkə ɔp me 'rutən]
to chop down	å felle	[ɔ 'fɛlə]
to deforest (vt)	å hogge ned	[ɔ 'hɔgə 'ne]
tree stump	stubbe (m)	['stʉbə]

campfire	bål (n)	['bɔl]
forest fire	skogbrann (m)	['skʊg,bran]
to extinguish (vt)	å slokke	[ɔ 'ʂløkə]

forest ranger	skogvokter (m)	['skʊg,vɔktər]
protection	vern (n), beskyttelse (m)	['væ:n], [be'ʂytəlsə]
to protect (~ nature)	å beskytte	[ɔ be'ʂytə]
poacher	tyvskytter (m)	['tyf,ʂytər]
steel trap	saks (m/f)	['saks]

| to gather, to pick (vt) | å plukke | [ɔ 'plʉkə] |
| to lose one's way | å gå seg vill | [ɔ 'gɔ sæj 'vil] |

84. Natural resources

natural resources	naturressurser (m pl)	[na'tʉr rɛ'sʉşər]
minerals	mineraler (n pl)	[mine'ralər]
deposits	forekomster (m pl)	['forə,kɔmstər]
field (e.g. oilfield)	felt (m)	['fɛlt]

to mine (extract)	å utvinne	[ɔ 'ʉt,vinə]
mining (extraction)	utvinning (m/f)	['ʉt,viniŋ]
ore	malm (m)	['malm]
mine (e.g. for coal)	gruve (m/f)	['grʉvə]
shaft (mine ~)	gruvesjakt (m/f)	['grʉvə,ʂakt]
miner	gruvearbeider (m)	['grʉvə'ar,bæjdər]
gas (natural ~)	gass (m)	['gas]
gas pipeline	gassledning (m)	['gas,ledniŋ]

oil (petroleum)	olje (m)	['ɔljə]
oil pipeline	oljeledning (m)	['ɔljə‚ledniŋ]
oil well	oljebrønn (m)	['ɔljə‚brœn]
derrick (tower)	boretårn (n)	['bo:rə‚tɔ:ŋ]
tanker	tankskip (n)	['tɑnk‚ṣip]

sand	sand (m)	['sɑn]
limestone	kalkstein (m)	['kɑlk‚stæjn]
gravel	grus (m)	['grʉs]
peat	torv (m/f)	['tɔrv]
clay	leir (n)	['læjr]
coal	kull (n)	['kʉl]

iron (ore)	jern (n)	['jæ:ŋ]
gold	gull (n)	['gʉl]
silver	sølv (n)	['søl]
nickel	nikkel (m)	['nikəl]
copper	kobber (n)	['kɔbər]

zinc	sink (m/n)	['sink]
manganese	mangan (m/n)	[mɑ'ŋɑn]
mercury	kvikksølv (n)	['kvik‚søl]
lead	bly (n)	['bly]

mineral	mineral (n)	[minə'rɑl]
crystal	krystall (m/n)	[kry'stɑl]
marble	marmor (m/n)	['mɑrmʉr]
uranium	uran (m/n)	[ʉ'rɑn]

85. Weather

weather	vær (n)	['vær]
weather forecast	værvarsel (n)	['vær‚vaṣəl]
temperature	temperatur (m)	[tɛmpərɑ'tʉr]
thermometer	termometer (n)	[tɛrmʉ'metər]
barometer	barometer (n)	[bɑrʉ'metər]

humid (adj)	fuktig	['fʉkti]
humidity	fuktighet (m)	['fʉkti‚het]
heat (extreme ~)	hete (m)	['he:tə]
hot (torrid)	het	['het]
it's hot	det er hett	[de ær 'het]

| it's warm | det er varmt | [de ær 'vɑrmt] |
| warm (moderately hot) | varm | ['vɑrm] |

| it's cold | det er kaldt | [de ær 'kɑlt] |
| cold (adj) | kald | ['kɑl] |

sun	sol (m/f)	['sʉl]
to shine (vi)	å skinne	[ɔ 'ṣinə]
sunny (day)	solrik	['sʉl‚rik]
to come up (vi)	å gå opp	[ɔ 'gɔ ɔp]
to set (vi)	å gå ned	[ɔ 'gɔ ne]

cloud	sky (m)	['şy]
cloudy (adj)	skyet	['şy:ət]
rain cloud	regnsky (m/f)	['ræjn‚şy]
somber (gloomy)	mørk	['mœrk]

rain	regn (n)	['ræjn]
it's raining	det regner	[de 'ræjnər]
rainy (~ day, weather)	regnværs-	['ræjn‚væş-]
to drizzle (vi)	å småregne	[ɔ 'smo:ræjnə]

pouring rain	piskende regn (n)	['piskenə ‚ræjn]
downpour	styrtregn (n)	['sty:t‚ræjn]
heavy (e.g. ~ rain)	kraftig, sterk	['krɑfti], ['stærk]
puddle	vannpytt (m)	['vɑn‚pyt]
to get wet (in rain)	å bli våt	[ɔ 'bli 'vɔt]

fog (mist)	tåke (m/f)	['to:kə]
foggy	tåke	['to:kə]
snow	snø (m)	['snø]
it's snowing	det snør	[de 'snør]

86. Severe weather. Natural disasters

thunderstorm	tordenvær (n)	['turdən‚vær]
lightning (~ strike)	lyn (n)	['lyn]
to flash (vi)	å glimte	[ɔ 'glimtə]

thunder	torden (m)	['turdən]
to thunder (vi)	å tordne	[ɔ 'turdnə]
it's thundering	det tordner	[de 'turdnər]

| hail | hagle (m/f) | ['hɑglə] |
| it's hailing | det hagler | [de 'hɑglər] |

| to flood (vt) | å oversvømme | [ɔ 'ovə‚svœmə] |
| flood, inundation | oversvømmelse (m) | ['ovə‚svœməlsə] |

earthquake	jordskjelv (n)	['ju:r‚şɛlv]
tremor, quake	skjelv (n)	['şɛlv]
epicentre	episenter (n)	[ɛpi'sɛntər]

| eruption | utbrudd (n) | ['ʉt‚brʉd] |
| lava | lava (m) | ['lɑvɑ] |

twister	skypumpe (m/f)	['şy‚pʉmpə]
tornado	tornado (m)	[tʊ:'nɑdʊ]
typhoon	tyfon (m)	[ty'fʊn]

hurricane	orkan (m)	[ɔr'kɑn]
storm	storm (m)	['stɔrm]
tsunami	tsunami (m)	[tsʉ'nɑmi]

| cyclone | syklon (m) | [sy'klun] |
| bad weather | uvær (n) | ['ʉ:‚vær] |

fire (accident)	**brann** (m)	['brɑn]
disaster	**katastrofe** (m)	[kɑtɑ'strɔfə]
meteorite	**meteoritt** (m)	[meteʊ'rit]
avalanche	**lavine** (m)	[lɑ'vinə]
snowslide	**snøskred, snøras** (n)	['snø,skred], ['snørɑs]
blizzard	**snøstorm** (m)	['snø,stɔrm]
snowstorm	**snøstorm** (m)	['snø,stɔrm]

FAUNA

87. Mammals. Predators

predator	rovdyr (n)	['rɔv‚dyr]
tiger	tiger (m)	['tigər]
lion	løve (m/f)	['løve]
wolf	ulv (m)	['ʉlv]
fox	rev (m)	['rev]
jaguar	jaguar (m)	[jagʉ'ar]
leopard	leopard (m)	[leʉ'pard]
cheetah	gepard (m)	[ge'pard]
black panther	panter (m)	['pantər]
puma	puma (m)	['pʉma]
snow leopard	snøleopard (m)	['snø leʉ'pard]
lynx	gaupe (m/f)	['gaʉpə]
coyote	coyote, prærieulv (m)	[kɔ'jotə], ['præri‚ʉlv]
jackal	sjakal (m)	[ʂa'kal]
hyena	hyene (m)	[hy'enə]

88. Wild animals

animal	dyr (n)	['dyr]
beast (animal)	best, udyr (n)	['bɛst], ['ʉ‚dyr]
squirrel	ekorn (n)	['ɛkʉːn]
hedgehog	pinnsvin (n)	['pin‚svin]
hare	hare (m)	['harə]
rabbit	kanin (m)	[ka'nin]
badger	grevling (m)	['grɛvliŋ]
raccoon	vaskebjørn (m)	['vaskə‚bjœːŋ]
hamster	hamster (m)	['hamstər]
marmot	murmeldyr (n)	['mʉrmel‚dyr]
mole	muldvarp (m)	['mʉl‚varp]
mouse	mus (m/f)	['mʉs]
rat	rotte (m/f)	['rotə]
bat	flaggermus (m/f)	['flagər‚mʉs]
ermine	røyskatt (m)	['røjskat]
sable	sobel (m)	['sʉbəl]
marten	mår (m)	['mɔr]
weasel	snømus (m/f)	['snø‚mʉs]
mink	mink (m)	['mink]

| beaver | bever (m) | ['bevər] |
| otter | oter (m) | ['ʊtər] |

horse	hest (m)	['hɛst]
moose	elg (m)	['ɛlg]
deer	hjort (m)	['jɔ:t]
camel	kamel (m)	[ka'mel]

bison	bison (m)	['bisɔn]
aurochs	urokse (m)	['ʉr͵ʊksə]
buffalo	bøffel (m)	['bøfəl]

zebra	sebra (m)	['sebra]
antelope	antilope (m)	[anti'lʊpə]
roe deer	rådyr (n)	['rɔ͵dyr]
fallow deer	dåhjort, dådyr (n)	['dɔ͵jo:t], ['dɔ͵dyr]
chamois	gemse (m)	['gɛmsə]
wild boar	villsvin (n)	['vil͵svin]

whale	hval (m)	['val]
seal	sel (m)	['sel]
walrus	hvalross (m)	['val͵rɔs]
fur seal	pelssel (m)	['pɛls͵sel]
dolphin	delfin (m)	[dɛl'fin]

bear	bjørn (m)	['bjœ:ɳ]
polar bear	isbjørn (m)	['is͵bjœ:ɳ]
panda	panda (m)	['panda]

monkey	ape (m/f)	['ape]
chimpanzee	sjimpanse (m)	[ʂim'pansə]
orangutan	orangutang (m)	[ʊ'raŋgʉ͵taŋ]
gorilla	gorilla (m)	[gɔ'rila]
macaque	makak (m)	[ma'kak]
gibbon	gibbon (m)	['gibʊn]

elephant	elefant (m)	[ɛle'fant]
rhinoceros	neshorn (n)	['nes͵hʊ:ɳ]
giraffe	sjiraff (m)	[ʂi'raf]
hippopotamus	flodhest (m)	['flʊd͵hɛst]

| kangaroo | kenguru (m) | ['kɛŋgʉrʉ] |
| koala (bear) | koala (m) | [kʊ'ala] |

mongoose	mangust, mungo (m)	[maŋ'gʉst], ['mʉŋgu]
chinchilla	chinchilla (m)	[ʂin'ʂila]
skunk	skunk (m)	['skunk]
porcupine	hulepinnsvin (n)	['hʉlə͵pinsvin]

89. Domestic animals

cat	katt (m)	['kat]
tomcat	hannkatt (m)	['han͵kat]
dog	hund (m)	['hʉn]

horse	hest (m)	['hɛst]
stallion (male horse)	hingst (m)	['hiŋst]
mare	hoppe, merr (m/f)	['hɔpə], ['mɛr]

cow	ku (f)	['kʉ]
bull	tyr (m)	['tyr]
ox	okse (m)	['ɔksə]

sheep (ewe)	sau (m)	['saʊ]
ram	vær, saubukk (m)	['vær], ['saʊ,bʉk]
goat	geit (m/f)	['jæjt]
billy goat, he-goat	geitebukk (m)	['jæjtə,bʉk]

| donkey | esel (n) | ['ɛsəl] |
| mule | muldyr (n) | ['mʉl,dyr] |

pig	svin (n)	['svin]
piglet	gris (m)	['gris]
rabbit	kanin (m)	[ka'nin]

| hen (chicken) | høne (m/f) | ['hønə] |
| cock | hane (m) | ['hanə] |

duck	and (m/f)	['an]
drake	andrik (m)	['andrik]
goose	gås (m/f)	['gɔs]

| tom turkey, gobbler | kalkunhane (m) | [kal'kʉn,hanə] |
| turkey (hen) | kalkunhøne (m/f) | [kal'kʉn,hønə] |

domestic animals	husdyr (n pl)	['hʉs,dyr]
tame (e.g. ~ hamster)	tam	['tam]
to tame (vt)	å temme	[ɔ 'tɛmə]
to breed (vt)	å avle, å oppdrette	[ɔ 'avlə], [ɔ 'ɔp,drɛtə]

farm	farm, gård (m)	['farm], ['gɔːr]
poultry	fjærfe (n)	['fjær,fɛ]
cattle	kveg (n)	['kvɛg]
herd (cattle)	flokk, bøling (m)	['flɔk], ['bøliŋ]

stable	stall (m)	['stal]
pigsty	grisehus (n)	['grisə,hʉs]
cowshed	kufjøs (m/n)	['kʉ,fjøs]
rabbit hutch	kaninbur (n)	[ka'nin,bʉr]
hen house	hønsehus (n)	['hønsə,hʉs]

90. Birds

bird	fugl (m)	['fʉl]
pigeon	due (m/f)	['dʉə]
sparrow	spurv (m)	['spʉrv]
tit (great tit)	kjøttmeis (m/f)	['çœt,mæjs]
magpie	skjære (m/f)	['şærə]
raven	ravn (m)	['ravn]

crow	kråke (m)	['kro:kə]
jackdaw	kaie (m/f)	['kajə]
rook	kornkråke (m/f)	['kʊ:ŋ‚kro:kə]

duck	and (m/f)	['ɑn]
goose	gås (m/f)	['gɔs]
pheasant	fasan (m)	[fɑ'sɑn]

eagle	ørn (m/f)	['œ:ŋ]
hawk	hauk (m)	['haʊk]
falcon	falk (m)	['fɑlk]
vulture	gribb (m)	['grib]
condor (Andean ~)	kondor (m)	[kʊn'dʊr]

swan	svane (m/f)	['svɑnə]
crane	trane (m/f)	['trɑnə]
stork	stork (m)	['stɔrk]

parrot	papegøye (m)	[pɑpe'gøjə]
hummingbird	kolibri (m)	[kʊ'libri]
peacock	påfugl (m)	['pɔ‚fʉl]

ostrich	struts (m)	['strʉts]
heron	hegre (m)	['hæejrə]
flamingo	flamingo (m)	[flɑ'mingʊ]
pelican	pelikan (m)	[peli'kɑn]

| nightingale | nattergal (m) | ['nɑtər‚gɑl] |
| swallow | svale (m/f) | ['svɑlə] |

thrush	trost (m)	['trʊst]
song thrush	måltrost (m)	['mo:l‚trʊst]
blackbird	svarttrost (m)	['svɑ:‚trʊst]

swift	tårnseiler (m), tårnsvale (m/f)	['tɔ:ŋ‚sæejlə], ['tɔ:ŋ‚svɑlə]
lark	lerke (m/f)	['lærkə]
quail	vaktel (m)	['vɑktəl]

woodpecker	hakkespett (m)	['hɑkə‚spɛt]
cuckoo	gjøk, gauk (m)	['jøk], ['gaʊk]
owl	ugle (m/f)	['ʉglə]
eagle owl	hubro (m)	['hʉbrʊ]
wood grouse	storfugl (m)	['stʊr‚fʉl]
black grouse	orrfugl (m)	['ɔr‚fʉl]
partridge	rapphøne (m/f)	['rɑp‚hønə]

starling	stær (m)	['stær]
canary	kanarifugl (m)	[kɑ'nɑri‚fʉl]
hazel grouse	jerpe (m/f)	['jærpə]

| chaffinch | bokfink (m) | ['bʊk‚fink] |
| bullfinch | dompap (m) | ['dʊmpɑp] |

seagull	måke (m/f)	['mo:kə]
albatross	albatross (m)	['ɑlbɑ‚trɔs]
penguin	pingvin (m)	[piŋ'vin]

91. Fish. Marine animals

bream	brasme (m/f)	['brɑsmə]
carp	karpe (m)	['kɑrpə]
perch	åbor (m)	['obor]
catfish	malle (m)	['mɑlə]
pike	gjedde (m/f)	['jɛdə]
salmon	laks (m)	['lɑks]
sturgeon	stør (m)	['stør]
herring	sild (m/f)	['sil]
Atlantic salmon	atlanterhavslaks (m)	[ɑt'lɑntərhɑfsˌlɑks]
mackerel	makrell (m)	[mɑ'krɛl]
flatfish	rødspette (m/f)	['røˌspɛtə]
zander, pike perch	gjørs (m)	['jøːʂ]
cod	torsk (m)	['toʂk]
tuna	tunfisk (m)	['tʉnˌfisk]
trout	ørret (m)	['øret]
eel	ål (m)	['ɔl]
electric ray	elektrisk rokke (m/f)	[ɛ'lektrisk ˌrɔkə]
moray eel	murene (m)	[mʉ'rɛnə]
piranha	piraja (m)	[pi'rɑjɑ]
shark	hai (m)	['hɑj]
dolphin	delfin (m)	[dɛl'fin]
whale	hval (m)	['vɑl]
crab	krabbe (m)	['krɑbə]
jellyfish	manet (m/f), meduse (m)	['mɑnet], [me'dʉsə]
octopus	blekksprut (m)	['blekˌsprʉt]
starfish	sjøstjerne (m/f)	['ʂøˌstjæːɳə]
sea urchin	sjøpinnsvin (n)	['ʂøː'pinˌsvin]
seahorse	sjøhest (m)	['ʂøˌhɛst]
oyster	østers (m)	['østəʂ]
prawn	reke (m/f)	['rekə]
lobster	hummer (m)	['hʉmər]
spiny lobster	langust (m)	[lɑŋ'gʉst]

92. Amphibians. Reptiles

snake	slange (m)	['slɑŋə]
venomous (snake)	giftig	['jifti]
viper	hoggorm, huggorm (m)	['hʉgˌorm], ['hʉgˌorm]
cobra	kobra (m)	['kʉbrɑ]
python	pyton (m)	['pytɔn]
boa	boaslange (m)	['bɔɑˌslɑŋə]
grass snake	snok (m)	['snʉk]

| rattle snake | klapperslange (m) | ['klapə‚slaŋə] |
| anaconda | anakonda (m) | [anaˈkɔnda] |

lizard	øgle (m/f)	[ˈøglə]
iguana	iguan (m)	[iguˈan]
monitor lizard	varan (n)	[vaˈran]
salamander	salamander (m)	[salaˈmandər]
chameleon	kameleon (m)	[kaməleˈʊn]
scorpion	skorpion (m)	[skɔrpiˈʊn]

turtle	skilpadde (m/f)	[ˈʂil‚padə]
frog	frosk (m)	[ˈfrɔsk]
toad	padde (m/f)	[ˈpadə]
crocodile	krokodille (m)	[krʊkəˈdilə]

93. Insects

insect	insekt (n)	[ˈinsɛkt]
butterfly	sommerfugl (m)	[ˈsɔmər‚fʉl]
ant	maur (m)	[ˈmaʊr]
fly	flue (m/f)	[ˈflʉə]
mosquito	mygg (m)	[ˈmyg]
beetle	bille (m)	[ˈbilə]

wasp	veps (m)	[ˈvɛps]
bee	bie (m/f)	[ˈbiə]
bumblebee	humle (m/f)	[ˈhʉmlə]
gadfly (botfly)	brems (m)	[ˈbrɛms]

| spider | edderkopp (m) | [ˈɛdər‚kɔp] |
| spider's web | edderkoppnett (n) | [ˈɛdərkɔp‚nɛt] |

dragonfly	øyenstikker (m)	[ˈøjən‚stikər]
grasshopper	gresshoppe (m/f)	[ˈgrɛs‚hɔpə]
moth (night butterfly)	nattsvermer (m)	[ˈnat‚sværmər]

cockroach	kakerlakk (m)	[kakəˈlak]
tick	flått, midd (m)	[ˈflɔt], [ˈmid]
flea	loppe (f)	[ˈlɔpə]
midge	knott (m)	[ˈknɔt]

locust	vandgresshoppe (m/f)	[ˈvan ˈgrɛs‚hɔpə]
snail	snegl (m)	[ˈsnæjl]
cricket	siriss (m)	[ˈsi‚ris]
firefly	ildflue (m/f), lysbille (m)	[ˈil‚flʉə], [ˈlys‚bilə]
ladybird	marihøne (m/f)	[ˈmari‚hønə]
cockchafer	oldenborre (f)	[ˈɔldən‚bɔrə]

leech	igle (m/f)	[ˈiglə]
caterpillar	sommerfugllarve (m/f)	[ˈsɔmərfʉl‚larvə]
earthworm	meitemark (m)	[ˈmæjtə‚mark]
larva	larve (m/f)	[ˈlarvə]

FLORA

94. Trees

tree	tre (n)	['trɛ]
deciduous (adj)	løv-	['løv-]
coniferous (adj)	bar-	['bɑr-]
evergreen (adj)	eviggrønt	['ɛvi‚grœnt]
apple tree	epletre (n)	['ɛplə‚trɛ]
pear tree	pæretre (n)	['pærə‚trɛ]
sweet cherry tree	morelltre (n)	[mʊ'rɛl‚trɛ]
sour cherry tree	kirsebærtre (n)	['çişəbær‚trɛ]
plum tree	plommetre (n)	['plʊmə‚trɛ]
birch	bjørk (f)	['bjœrk]
oak	eik (f)	['æjk]
linden tree	lind (m/f)	['lin]
aspen	osp (m/f)	['ɔsp]
maple	lønn (m/f)	['lœn]
spruce	gran (m/f)	['grɑn]
pine	furu (m/f)	['fʉrʉ]
larch	lerk (m)	['lærk]
fir tree	edelgran (m/f)	['ɛdəl‚grɑn]
cedar	seder (m)	['sedər]
poplar	poppel (m)	['pɔpəl]
rowan	rogn (m/f)	['rɔŋn]
willow	pil (m/f)	['pil]
alder	or, older (m/f)	['ʊr], ['ɔldər]
beech	bøk (m)	['bøk]
elm	alm (m)	['ɑlm]
ash (tree)	ask (m/f)	['ɑsk]
chestnut	kastanjetre (n)	[kɑ'stɑnje‚trɛ]
magnolia	magnolia (m)	[mɑŋ'nʊliɑ]
palm tree	palme (m)	['pɑlmə]
cypress	sypress (m)	[sʏ'prɛs]
mangrove	mangrove (m)	[mɑŋ'grʊvə]
baobab	apebrødtre (n)	['ɑpebrø‚trɛ]
eucalyptus	eukalyptus (m)	[ɛvkɑ'lyptʉs]
sequoia	sequoia (m)	['sek‚vɔjɑ]

95. Shrubs

bush	busk (m)	['bʉsk]
shrub	busk (m)	['bʉsk]

| grapevine | vinranke (m) | ['vin‚rankə] |
| vineyard | vinmark (m/f) | ['vin‚mark] |

raspberry bush	bringebærbusk (m)	['briŋə‚bær busk]
blackcurrant bush	solbærbusk (m)	['sulbær‚busk]
redcurrant bush	ripsbusk (m)	['rips‚busk]
gooseberry bush	stikkelsbærbusk (m)	['stikəlsbær‚busk]

acacia	akasie (m)	[a'kasiə]
barberry	berberis (m)	['bærberis]
jasmine	sjasmin (m)	[ʂas'min]

juniper	einer (m)	['æjnər]
rosebush	rosenbusk (m)	['rusən‚busk]
dog rose	steinnype (m/f)	['stæjn‚nypə]

96. Fruits. Berries

fruit	frukt (m/f)	['frukt]
fruits	frukter (m/f pl)	['fruktər]
apple	eple (n)	['ɛplə]
pear	pære (m/f)	['pærə]
plum	plomme (m/f)	['plumə]

strawberry (garden ~)	jordbær (n)	['ju:r‚bær]
sour cherry	kirsebær (n)	['çiʂə‚bær]
sweet cherry	morell (m)	[mu'rɛl]
grape	drue (m)	['druə]

raspberry	bringebær (n)	['briŋə‚bær]
blackcurrant	solbær (n)	['sul‚bær]
redcurrant	rips (m)	['rips]
gooseberry	stikkelsbær (n)	['stikəls‚bær]
cranberry	tranebær (n)	['tranə‚bær]

orange	appelsin (m)	[apel'sin]
tangerine	mandarin (m)	[manda'rin]
pineapple	ananas (m)	['ananas]

| banana | banan (m) | [ba'nan] |
| date | daddel (m) | ['dadəl] |

lemon	sitron (m)	[si'trun]
apricot	aprikos (m)	[apri'kus]
peach	fersken (m)	['fæʂkən]

| kiwi | kiwi (m) | ['kivi] |
| grapefruit | grapefrukt (m/f) | ['grɛjp‚frukt] |

berry	bær (n)	['bær]
berries	bær (n pl)	['bær]
cowberry	tyttebær (n)	['tʏtə‚bær]
wild strawberry	markjordbær (n)	['mark ju:r‚bær]
bilberry	blåbær (n)	['blɔ‚bær]

97. Flowers. Plants

flower	blomst (m)	['blɔmst]
bouquet (of flowers)	bukett (m)	[bʉ'kɛt]
rose (flower)	rose (m/f)	['rʉsə]
tulip	tulipan (m)	[tʉli'pɑn]
carnation	nellik (m)	['nɛlik]
gladiolus	gladiolus (m)	[glɑdi'ɔlʉs]
cornflower	kornblomst (m)	['kʊːn̩ˌblɔmst]
harebell	blåklokke (m/f)	['blɔˌklɔkə]
dandelion	løvetann (m/f)	['løvəˌtɑn]
camomile	kamille (m)	[kɑ'milə]
aloe	aloe (m)	['ɑlʊe]
cactus	kaktus (m)	['kɑktʉs]
rubber plant, ficus	gummiplante (m/f)	['gʉmiˌplɑntə]
lily	lilje (m)	['liljə]
geranium	geranium (m)	[ge'rɑnium]
hyacinth	hyasint (m)	[hiɑ'sint]
mimosa	mimose (m/f)	[mi'mɔsə]
narcissus	narsiss (m)	[nɑ'ʂis]
nasturtium	blomkarse (m)	['blɔmˌkɑʂə]
orchid	orkidé (m)	[ɔrki'de]
peony	peon, pion (m)	[pe'ʊn], [pi'ʊn]
violet	fiol (m)	[fi'ʊl]
pansy	stemorsblomst (m)	['stemʉʂˌblɔmst]
forget-me-not	forglemmegei (m)	[fɔr'gleməˌjæj]
daisy	tusenfryd (m)	['tʉsənˌfryd]
poppy	valmue (m)	['vɑlmʉe]
hemp	hamp (m)	['hɑmp]
mint	mynte (m/f)	['mʏntə]
lily of the valley	liljekonvall (m)	['liljə kɔn'vɑl]
snowdrop	snøklokke (m/f)	['snøˌklɔkə]
nettle	nesle (m/f)	['nɛslə]
sorrel	syre (m/f)	['syrə]
water lily	nøkkerose (m/f)	['nøkeˌrʉse]
fern	bregne (m/f)	['brɛjnə]
lichen	lav (m/n)	['lɑv]
greenhouse (tropical ~)	drivhus (n)	['drivˌhʉs]
lawn	gressplen (m)	['grɛsˌplen]
flowerbed	blomsterbed (n)	['blɔmstərˌbed]
plant	plante (m/f), vekst (m)	['plɑntə], ['vɛkst]
grass	gras (n)	['grɑs]
blade of grass	grasstrå (n)	['grɑsˌstrɔ]

leaf	blad (n)	['bla]
petal	kronblad (n)	['krɔnˌbla]
stem	stilk (m)	['stilk]
tuber	rotknoll (m)	['rʊtˌknɔl]

| young plant (shoot) | spire (m/f) | ['spirə] |
| thorn | torn (m) | ['tʊːn̩] |

to blossom (vi)	å blomstre	[ɔ 'blɔmstrə]
to fade, to wither	å visne	[ɔ 'visnə]
smell (odour)	lukt (m/f)	['lʉkt]
to cut (flowers)	å skjære av	[ɔ 'ʂæːrə aː]
to pick (a flower)	å plukke	[ɔ 'plʉkə]

98. Cereals, grains

grain	korn (n)	['kʊːn̩]
cereal crops	cerealer (n pl)	[sere'alər]
ear (of barley, etc.)	aks (n)	['aks]

wheat	hvete (m)	['vetə]
rye	rug (m)	['rʉg]
oats	havre (m)	['havrə]
millet	hirse (m)	['hiʂə]
barley	bygg (m/n)	['bʏg]

maize	mais (m)	['mais]
rice	ris (m)	['ris]
buckwheat	bokhvete (m)	['bʊkˌvetə]

pea plant	ert (m/f)	['æːt]
kidney bean	bønne (m/f)	['bœnə]
soya	soya (m)	['sɔja]
lentil	linse (m/f)	['linsə]
beans (pulse crops)	bønner (m/f pl)	['bœnər]

COUNTRIES OF THE WORLD

99. Countries. Part 1

Afghanistan	**Afghanistan**	[afˈɡaniˌstan]
Albania	**Albania**	[alˈbania]
Argentina	**Argentina**	[arɡɛnˈtina]
Armenia	**Armenia**	[arˈmenia]
Australia	**Australia**	[auˈstralia]
Austria	**Østerrike**	[ˈøstəˌrikə]
Azerbaijan	**Aserbajdsjan**	[aserbajdˈʂan]
The Bahamas	**Bahamas**	[baˈhamas]
Bangladesh	**Bangladesh**	[banglaˈdɛʂ]
Belarus	**Hviterussland**	[ˈvitəˌrʉslan]
Belgium	**Belgia**	[ˈbɛlgia]
Bolivia	**Bolivia**	[bɔˈlivia]
Bosnia and Herzegovina	**Bosnia-Hercegovina**	[ˈbosnia herseɡɔˌvina]
Brazil	**Brasilia**	[braˈsilia]
Bulgaria	**Bulgaria**	[bʉlˈgaria]
Cambodia	**Kambodsja**	[kamˈbɔdʂa]
Canada	**Canada**	[ˈkanada]
Chile	**Chile**	[ˈtʂilə]
China	**Kina**	[ˈçina]
Colombia	**Colombia**	[kɔˈlʉmbia]
Croatia	**Kroatia**	[krʉˈatia]
Cuba	**Cuba**	[ˈkʉba]
Cyprus	**Kypros**	[ˈkyprʉs]
Czech Republic	**Tsjekkia**	[ˈtʂɛkija]
Denmark	**Danmark**	[ˈdanmark]
Dominican Republic	**Dominikanske Republikken**	[dʉminiˈkanskə repʉˈblikən]
Ecuador	**Ecuador**	[ɛkʉaˈdɔr]
Egypt	**Egypt**	[ɛˈgypt]
England	**England**	[ˈɛŋlan]
Estonia	**Estland**	[ˈɛstlan]
Finland	**Finland**	[ˈfinlan]
France	**Frankrike**	[ˈfrankrikə]
French Polynesia	**Fransk Polynesia**	[ˈfransk polyˈnesia]
Georgia	**Georgia**	[geˈɔrgia]
Germany	**Tyskland**	[ˈtysklan]
Ghana	**Ghana**	[ˈgana]
Great Britain	**Storbritannia**	[ˈstʉr briˌtania]
Greece	**Hellas**	[ˈhɛlas]
Haiti	**Haiti**	[haˈiti]
Hungary	**Ungarn**	[ˈʉŋaːn]

100. Countries. Part 2

Iceland	Island	['islɑn]
India	India	['indiɑ]
Indonesia	Indonesia	[indʊ'nesiɑ]
Iran	Iran	['irɑn]
Iraq	Irak	['irɑk]
Ireland	Irland	['irlɑn]
Israel	Israel	['isrɑəl]
Italy	Italia	[i'tɑliɑ]
Jamaica	Jamaica	[ṣɑ'mɑjkɑ]
Japan	Japan	['jɑpɑn]
Jordan	Jordan	['jɔrdɑn]
Kazakhstan	Kasakhstan	[kɑ'sɑk‚stɑn]
Kenya	Kenya	['kenyɑ]
Kirghizia	Kirgisistan	[kir'gisi‚stɑn]
Kuwait	Kuwait	['kʉvɑjt]
Laos	Laos	['lɑɔs]
Latvia	Latvia	['lɑtviɑ]
Lebanon	Libanon	['libɑnɔn]
Libya	Libya	['libiɑ]
Liechtenstein	Liechtenstein	['lihtɛnʂtæjn]
Lithuania	Litauen	['li‚tɑʊən]
Luxembourg	Luxembourg	['lʉksɛm‚bʉrg]
Macedonia (Republic of ~)	Makedonia	[mɑke'dɔniɑ]
Madagascar	Madagaskar	[mɑdɑ'gɑskɑr]
Malaysia	Malaysia	[mɑ'lɑjsiɑ]
Malta	Malta	['mɑltɑ]
Mexico	Mexico	['mɛksikʉ]
Moldova, Moldavia	Moldova	[mɔl'dɔvɑ]
Monaco	Monaco	[mʊ'nɑkʉ]
Mongolia	Mongolia	[mʊŋ'guliɑ]
Montenegro	Montenegro	['mɔntə‚nɛgrʉ]
Morocco	Marokko	[mɑ'rɔkʉ]
Myanmar	Myanmar	['mjænmɑ]
Namibia	Namibia	[nɑ'mibiɑ]
Nepal	Nepal	['nepɑl]
Netherlands	Nederland	['nedə‚lɑn]
New Zealand	New Zealand	[njʉ'selɑn]
North Korea	Nord-Korea	['nʉːr kʉ'rɛɑ]
Norway	Norge	['nɔrgə]

101. Countries. Part 3

Pakistan	Pakistan	['pɑki‚stɑn]
Palestine	Palestina	[pɑle'stinɑ]
Panama	Panama	['pɑnɑmɑ]
Paraguay	Paraguay	[pɑrɑg'wɑj]

Peru	Peru	[pe'ruː]
Poland	Polen	['pʊlen]
Portugal	Portugal	[pɔːtʉ'gal]
Romania	Romania	[rʊ'manіa]
Russia	Russland	['rʉslɑn]

Saudi Arabia	Saudi-Arabia	['saʊdi ɑ'rɑbia]
Scotland	Skottland	['skɔtlɑn]
Senegal	Senegal	[sene'gal]
Serbia	Serbia	['særbia]
Slovakia	Slovakia	[ʂlʊ'vakia]
Slovenia	Slovenia	[ʂlʊ'venia]

South Africa	Republikken Sør-Afrika	[repʉ'bliken 'sør͵afrikɑ]
South Korea	Sør-Korea	['sør kʊ͵rea]
Spain	Spania	['spania]
Suriname	Surinam	['sʉri͵nam]
Sweden	Sverige	['sværiə]
Switzerland	Sveits	['svæjts]
Syria	Syria	['syria]

Taiwan	Taiwan	['taj͵van]
Tajikistan	Tadsjikistan	[tɑ'dʂiki͵stan]
Tanzania	Tanzania	['tansɑ͵nia]
Tasmania	Tasmania	[tas'mania]
Thailand	Thailand	['tajlɑn]
Tunisia	Tunisia	['tʉ'nisia]
Turkey	Tyrkia	[tyrkia]
Turkmenistan	Turkmenistan	[tʉrk'meni͵stan]

Ukraine	Ukraina	[ʉkrɑ'ina]
United Arab Emirates	Forente Arabiske Emiratene	[fɔ'rente ɑ'rabiskə ɛmi'ratenə]
United States of America	Amerikas Forente Stater	[ɑ'merikas fɔ'rɛntə 'statər]
Uruguay	Uruguay	[ʉrygʊ'aj]
Uzbekistan	Usbekistan	[ʉs'beki͵stan]

Vatican	Vatikanet	['vati͵kane]
Venezuela	Venezuela	[venesʉ'ɛla]
Vietnam	Vietnam	['vjɛtnam]
Zanzibar	Zanzibar	['sansibar]

www.ingramcontent.com/pod-product-compliance
Lightning Source LLC
Chambersburg PA
CBHW070823050426
42452CB00011B/2156